100 POEMS
TO MAKE YOU
TLC
THINK, LAUGH & CRY

100 Poems to make you TLC

Spiderwize
Remus House
Coltsfoot Drive
Woodston
Peterborough
PE2 9BF

www.spiderwize.com

A CIP catalogue record for this book is available from the British Library.

ISBN: 978-1-911596-05-9
Ebook ISBN: 978-1-911596-06-6

100 POEMS
TO MAKE YOU
TLC
THINK, LAUGH & CRY

ANDREW EVZONA

FOREWORD

These 100 poems are about personal matters and life matters and were written from the heart and took barely 5-10 minutes to compose.

I hope they really do make you "think, laugh and cry", and thank you for your kind donations to both Diabetes and Cancer Research who will receive a pound for every book sold.

Some poems have already been featured in various anthologies by Forward Poetry and are highlighted accordingly.

CONTENTS

THINK

LAUGH

CRY

THINK

The Queen
Written 18th December 2014

God save the Queen
Her Majesty in her glory
A lifetime of responsibility
And her never-ending story

She ascended to the throne
At a very tender age
With her husband by her side
As she walked the world's stage

Everywhere she went
So many smiling faces
Some giving her presents
I saw her at Ascot races

She always moves with grace
No matter where she goes
She has served her subjects well
Through the highs and the lows

She has feelings too
Her annus horribilis felt by all
The sadness and the scandal
As the flag flies over Windsor Castle

So many events to attend to
The trooping of the colour and Remembrance Day
She travels the world over
Certainly hard work and not much play

And as 2015 approaches
A landmark awaits Her Majesty
On 10th September she surpasses
Victoria's length of reign for all to see

She is proud of her children
For raising their own family
To protect the distant future
Of our well-respected monarchy

So God save the Queen
Let she live to make a hundred
May her final years be more peaceful
She will be long remembered after she's dead

BUCKINGHAM PALACE

13ᵗʰ July 2015.

Dear Mr Evzona,

The Queen wishes me to write and thank you for your poem.

Her Majesty greatly appreciates the sentiments you express in your verses and, although unable to reply to you personally, The Queen thought it was kind of you to compose your poem especially for Her Majesty in her Diamond Jubilee year.

Yours sincerely

Mary Morrison.

Lady-in-Waiting

Mr A Evzona

Time

Written 2nd October 2012
Published in End of Days – A Collection of Poetry

Who invented time, and do we know why?
Was it really the bearded man above in the sky?
Does it really matter whether it is day or night
And whether the time is wrong or right?

We work and sleep, and love to play
As time ticks on, whether we are home or away
We're born so vulnerable, and bring so much joy
To our parents and family, whether we are a girl or a boy

They watch us grow, no matter how big or small
And love us the same, if we're short or tall
And they laugh and cry, hoping we will try
To fulfill their dreams for us, before they die

Time waits for no-one, as we all know
We must always take care, wherever we go
There are those who are lucky, and know little pain
Whilst others may suffer, again and again

So just live your lives, as best you can
As you grow, into a woman or a man
Remember there is nothing certain in this life
Even for those, who are husband and wife

And as we draw our very last breath
We may wonder, 'is there life after death?'
As our family grieve, and tears run down their face
Maybe we all will have gone, to a far better place

Reflections
Written 15th March 2007

When we look out of the window, do we ask where
Or if we'll be here in a hundred years, or do we, really, care?
I fear the worst awaits us all,
Maybe ignorance is bliss,
Was it really an act of God,
That created all of this?

Maybe just like me, you're all alone
Even if you've family at home
To love and be loved, is this true?
Look around, are you so sure?
That every person feels secure
Even from the day you say 'I do'

Children can be heard and seen
Happy laughter, clothes so clean
Too young to understand, life elsewhere
Where an evil mind can make them cry
No tears of joy, don't ask them why
Just fear and famine and a prayer

When you wake, treat every day as your last
Greet the future, but don't forget the past
Accept all life's problems with humility
There, but for the grace of God, go you and me
The blind, the deaf, the dumb, all who suffer
Remember, none of us is better than any other

Why?
Written 4th October 2012

Why do babies always cry....why?
Why do clouds stay in the sky....why?
Why do we have to go to school....why?
Why do we have to obey the rule....why?
Why do children shout and fight....why?
Why is a teacher always right....why?

Why do we have a husband and wife....why?
Why do we eat with a fork and knife....why?
Why do we consume or drink to excess....why?
Why do some get in a mess....why?
Why does anyone ever smoke....why?
Why can't so many take a joke....why?

Why do we have to work to be paid....why?
Why do some lucky ones have it made...why?
Why do some shop all day long....why?
Why do we vote for who's right or wrong....why?
Why do cars, trains and planes crash....why?
Why is there thunder, and lightning flash....why?

Why does anyone, take another's life away....why?
Why so many religions, to cope with every day...why?
Why are there wars and so much hunger too....why?
Why do some suffer, their whole life through....why?
Why are we here, and will we ever know....why?
Why do all of us, eventually, have to go....why?

Disability

Written 31st October 2012

Why are so many, born with a disability?
Why aren't we all the same?
They live their lives, don't seek our pity
Though for them, we feel the pain

They need constant attention, as we try to make sure
No further misfortunes come their way
The frustrations are the same, whether rich or poor
Please find a cure, to our creator we pray

Those who know no different, carry on regardless
Each day they are used to their plight
Whilst all life's challenges can give them extra stress
Though they never give up the fight

There are others who are struck with it, later in life
A shock which no-one can ever explain
If they're married they need love and care from husband or wife
As the family cope with the strain

So those of us lucky to have all our faculties
Should remember that life is not always normal
Take care where you go, say thank you and please
Disability could come to us all

nown

ecretion

cardiovascular

produced

relatively

omplicatio

necessary

sitivity

reas sugar

beta high m

iab

Good Health
Written 11th October 2012

Please let us have good health, no more sneezes
Or coughs, temperatures and terrible wheezes
Drink plenty of water and eat fruit and veg too
Always be diligent in everything you do

Try to keep those nasty, little germs away
Make sure you wash your hands thoroughly every day
Dress for the weather and not just for show
With your wits about you, wherever you go

If the flesh is willing, but the body is weak
Just stay in bed, recover, there's always next week
Always throw away tissues that you have used
Be thoughtful about others, you won't be abused

Your body is your temple, from birth until the end
Look after it and treat it as your very best friend
No smoking, no substances, and drink within reason
No excuses offered, whatever the season

Remember a smile is always better than a frown
Be strong and never let any illness bring you down
Time is the healer and you can stay well
Live your life sensibly until the final bell

CANC

ESTABLISHING

ATOPOIETIC

MO

EATMENTS

COM

IES

ONCOGENES

LOSS

PATHOGENE

IMAGING

EXTENT

MUTATE

DRUGS

OGIC

GROW

BLES

TYPICALLY

Heroes

Written 11th October 2012

Do we take our heroes for granted, or do we even care?
They come to our rescue, night and day, almost everywhere
From birth as our mother is in labour, feeling all the pain
The nurses and midwives are there to help, take away the strain

As we grow up and go to school, where we may play the fool
The teacher is there to help us through and understand the rule
If we are victims of an accident or critically ill
The doctors try their very best to keep us alive still

Our firemen put their lives at risk, no matter how severe
If there's a fire and we all panic, and for our lives may fear
And if we're threatened, mugged or attacked, on whom can we depend?
Our police will do their best to catch the culprit in the end

In times of war just who amongst us really wants to go
And risk their lives to keep us safe and fight against the foe
Our soldiers we know have no choice, no matter where they roam
We fear for them as many, for sure, will never return home

So please think of our heroes, always there for us in our need
The volunteers who help the suffering and those who cannot read
Let's praise their efforts in never shirking, they always try to cope
With what they're faced with, in every way, to give mankind some hope

Sleep

Written 29th August 2014
Published in Whispering Words
- A Collection of Poetry 31.01.15

Isn't it strange, from the moment we're born
How we need to sleep
Some of us merely sleeping light
While others far more deep

Eight hours is the ideal
You'll hear the doctors say
Don't try to fight it
Just relax and drift away

It really is a mystery
How we have a dream
Pleasurably or in pain
Though not always what it may seem

Some sleep with eyes shut tight
And others open slightly
But far away from the world
Trying not to sleep lightly

No-one likes to be woken
So suddenly their heart misses a beat
And most of all we prefer
Not to sleep in the cold or heat

Never take sleep for granted
No matter where you are
Some sleep in the strangest places
On a beach, in a train or car

Some enjoy their greatest fantasies
In the land of nod
Winning the lottery or just having fun
And maybe dreaming of God

So be sure to get enough shut-eye
Wherever you lay down your head
Sleep is just a part of life
As important as it is to be fed

Water
Written 30th October 2012

Our bodies are made up of it, water gives life to all
You all need to drink it, whether you're big or small
You can never take it for granted, especially when there's a drought
And using it every day, inside the home and out

It serves so many purposes, not just to wash and drink
And whenever you are using it, do you ever think?
Of all those who have suffered, when needing it the most
And those who are blessed, in the name of father, son and holy ghost

The relief you feel when you drink it, when the weather is too hot
Or when you use it for tea or coffee, pouring it in the pot
Some like it hot, and others prefer it cold
Everyone relies on it, no matter how young or old

The very word 'water' brings us so much hope
If we never had it how would we ever cope?
So do your heart a favour and drink 2 litres a day
Make water your priority, whether at work or play

Winners

Written 29th October 2012

Who are the real winners, you may well ask?
All who achieve their aim, no matter the task
From birth to old age, there are chances galore
To be a winner, and if you are you always want more

A mother is the first winner, when her child is born
Whilst those who hunger celebrate, when a harvest brings them corn
As a child grows and slowly knows, all that lies ahead
To pass exams, fulfill their potential, earn their crust of bread

To win the race, reach first place, in any sport or game
A winner is proud if they're the very best, their life is never the same
Everyone appreciates a talent which is supreme
So never give up and persevere, you can really live your dream

They say it's not the winning, what really counts is the taking part
Though if at first you happen to fail, try never to lose heart
Determination is the key, no matter what the cause
Practice makes perfect, always be fair and play within the laws

And remember those less fortunate, who never get the chance
They cannot run, jump or compete, in any game or dance
They are still winners all the same, the blind, the deaf, the poor
And those with missing limbs as well, never envy them for sure

Sprinter Sacre
Written 27th March 2013

It was fifty years ago
I first set eyes on my boyhood hero
Arkle was his name
And he was set for immortal fame

He thrilled us with his speed
And took on every deed
Carrying the heaviest of weight
He was the punter's best mate

And won 22 of 26 steeplechases
He tried his heart out in all his races
A joy to watch with Pat Taaffe on board
He put his opponents to the sword

And fifty years on another star
Has emerged who could be on a par
Sprinter Sacre has begun his reign
Already known as the Black Aeroplane

He cruises round at his leisure
And Barry Geraghty has the pleasure
Of steering him over each fence
Whilst Nicky Henderson watches so tense

He is such a joy to behold
And his opponents slowly but surely fold
To his prowess from another time
Always far ahead at the finish line

Let's hope for many years to come
For a horse who knows he's number one
In looks and speed and flight
He's my hero now alright

Arkle (Pat Taaffe) at Kempton Park on the day of his final
race, 27 December 1966.

Horses

Written 18th November 2013
Published in Animal Antics 2013

They have been with us from the very start
Our four-legged friends with the biggest heart
They come in all sizes, colours and shades
And our feelings for them, never fades

They've been used, in so many different ways
As they stood in fields, and enjoyed to graze
At first just to take us far and wide
We'd climb on top and just enjoy the ride

Then they were needed to carry our goods
Few could cope without wearing hoods
Sometimes carrying so much you could feel the strain
Was it fair they should endure so much pain?

Though worse was to come, as they served us in war
So many died, and those injured were more
It wasn't their fight, yet they were expected to charge
And take on the enemy, whether little or large

The thoroughbred was created to purely race
Against each other to secure their best place
Champions emerged, worth fortunes galore
But some owners were greedy, always wanting more

They raced on the flat and jumped fences too
They were expected to compete until their career was through
Many sent to stud, to continue this sport
Did they have any choice? No-one gave it a thought

Though better to live and die naturally
Than be shot for someone's lunch or tea
The horse is a creature of kings and queens
Respect and appreciate one of life's greatest beings

The Human Body
Written 28th July 2016

The human body is a fascination
From the moment it is conceived
Merely an embryo to begin with
When the baby arrives we are much relieved

The head is the main point of focus
With our eyes, ears, mouth and nose
Our body can be a various shape
All the way down to our toes

When we study biology at school
We see what we are made of inside
So many bones and vessels everywhere
Though we all look so different outside

We really are very brittle indeed
So many organs which need care
If something goes wrong we need a surgeon's skill
To have a lifetime without mishap is so rare

There are the alternative genders we know
As males and females are so different
All I can say is I'm glad I was born a male
As I could never have coped with being pregnant

Those who live until aged seventy and beyond
Experience all life's aches and pains
We are a most interesting species like no other
Though undoubtedly have the greatest brains

Human Nature
Written 28th July 2016

Human nature is full of various behaviour patterns
How do we decide how we'll behave and why?
Will we respect our parents and the right way to be?
Will we always tell the truth or sometimes lie?

We can laugh, we can cry, we can just be quiet
There are so many emotions which have their place
We can be friendly or angry, be good or bad
It is sad when there are some who are two-faced

We suffer stress and sometimes are driven to the very edge
By family, friends or even strangers too
At work with our colleagues, or team-mates in sport
Where some may cheat and we know they do

Relationships are always a test of our character
Better to love than hate anyone for sure
A hug or an embrace and tender loving care
The best remedy, as stress-prevention is better than a cure

Humans v Machines

Written 28th July 2016

Turn the clock back even just fifty years
And life was all so very different
We had choices of jobs and no redundancy fears
And there was no time like the present

Technology emerged and with it change
As computers came into play
Progressing rapidly in a various range
And time would give them a bigger say

Slowly man's jobs have been eroded far and wide
As machines are used more and more
Where will this lead to, and many have lost their pride
Unemployed, and maybe a future human-machine war

Who Are We?

Written 31st March 2014
*Published in Everlasting Words
– A Collection of Poetry*

We are the baby who cries
When we are born
We are the old person
Who dies and they mourn

We are the pupils
Who go to school to learn
We are the teachers
Ready to take our turn

We are the short
We are the tall
We are the big
We are the small

We are the happy
We are the sad
We are the sensible
We are the mad

We are the workers
Who have to earn our crust
We are the employers
Who must succeed or bust

We are the silent ones
Who think but never speak
We are the noisy ones
Who take advantage of the meek

We are the poor
Who struggle to make ends meet
We are the wealthy
Who have the world at our feet

We are the weak
Who suffer every day
We are the strong
And no-one gets in our way

We are the lonely
With no-one to turn to
We are the popular
With friends we never knew

We are the desperate
Who have to beg or steal
We are the thrifty
Whose lives remain unreal

We are the righteous
Who believe there is a God
We are the atheists
Who couldn't give a sod

We are the sheep
Who follow far behind
We are the leaders
Who control them with our mind

We know who we are
Wherever we may be
We're born, we live, we die
No matter who are we

Children
Written 14th June 2013

There was a time we were children, many years ago
Not a care in the world, no responsibilities, going to and fro
We'd laugh, skip, jump and run in the playground
Playing hide and seek too, hoping not to be found

Our lives were just beginning, we were so naive
Though there was nothing wrong in believing that we began with Adam and Eve
Our mum and dad looked after us, teaching us right and wrong
We were happy, mischievous, curious and sometimes burst into song

There was so much to learn about, as we started to explore
Pushed the boundaries as far as we could, always wanting more
Some were very lucky, received all their favourite toys
While others not so fortunate, the same for girls and boys

At Christmas time our eyes lit up, as we met Santa in his grotto
Would our wishes and dreams be satisfied? In those days there was no lotto
We were told to eat up all our greens, so that we might grow
Sometimes we argued with our parents, though they were right we know

Our childhood memories never fade, as we now look back
Playing football, running around. If we were naughty we'd get a smack
Scrumping was a favourite pastime, as we climbed up every tree
Reaching for those apples, hoping no-one would see

Though things today have changed so much. Where have the children gone?
So very few playing in the park, it was our second home
A world of technology has been thrust upon us, computers everywhere
Life is so different, though is it better, and do we really care?

Maybe it's just a phase of change and playing outdoors will return
Just like we did, no matter the weather, rain or sun burn
Children must be careful to act their age, and not grow up too fast
So, they too can remember their childhood, one day when it has past

Childhood

Written 3rd May 2007
Published in Off the Page
- A Collection of Poetry

It's great to be alive
At the tender age of five
No cares in the world for you
You believe everything is true

To run in the park and play
Look forward to every day
To just have lots of fun
Whether rain or cloud or sun

Learning all the time
Your favourite nursery rhyme
What to eat and drink
Always ready to think

Making friends anew
A host of things to do
Maybe have a dog or a cat
Or a tortoise, if you fancy that

Play games, indoors or out
Laugh and scream and shout
Be upset, if you're told off
Sometimes sneeze or cough

Enjoy these days for sure
Remember when you were four
As you grow tall and strong
Knowing what's right from wrong

Be your parents' pride and joy
As they buy your favourite toy
Let it be understood
You'll never forget your childhood

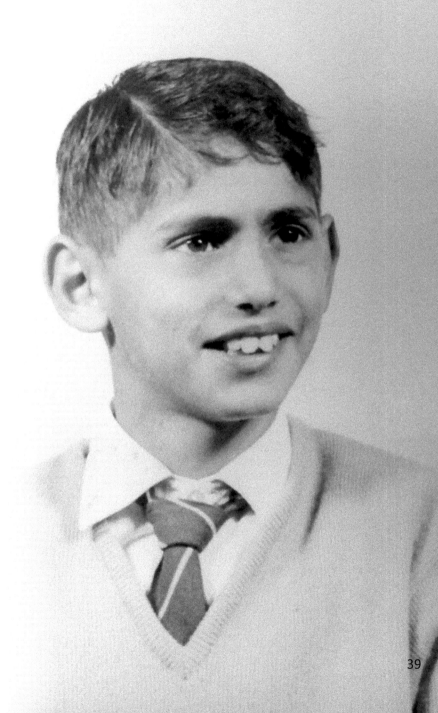

39

The Single, Married and Divorced Trilogy
Written 5th April 2016

Solitary
Individual
Narcissist
Guarded
Lonely
Empty

Matrimonial
Assimilated
Responsible
Repetitive
Ideal
Enthusiastic
Devoted

Divided
Irretrievable
Vicious
Obnoxious
Relieved
Catastrophic
Emancipated
Desperate

A Life of Birthdays
Written 8th March 2016

Our birthday is a special day
Though no-one knows their fate
Complications might set in
Hope they're found before it's too late

The first five years of our lives
Are when we watch and learn
From the behaviour of adults and older children
Then soon it is our turn

To become more demanding and scream and shout
Though not every child is the same
Some are quiet and others blow hot and cold
For a while life is just a game

By junior school we start to make friends
Some may remain with us for life
At senior school we are wiser still
May even meet a future husband or wife

Our teenage years can be a real challenge
As we take endless exams at school
Some succeed and some rebel
And some just play the fool

Eighteen is the first landmark
Nowadays the key to the door
Be careful when we celebrate
And don't end up on the floor

Our twenties are when we are on a high
As we work our way up the ladder
Interviews come and go, some in a secure job
Some not satisfied and some becoming madder

The thirties are a time to settle
Marry and start a family
Though it's a minefield to meet the right one
As there are many fish in the sea

The forties are supposed to be when life begins
As most are settled by then
Daily responsibilities and a routine
We know what to expect and when

The fifties is when experience counts
We have learned from previous mistakes
Some still married, others single or divorced
Forgive and forget for all our sakes

The sixties are our golden years
As retirement beckons for all
It's a bonus to be healthy, no aches or pains
Whether we are tall or small

The seventies are a time to reflect
On everything which has gone before
Some are grandparents by now
Giving advice on what they have seen and more

The eighties and older are when we are most at peace
Whether with family, a nursing home or alone
Some may still be active while others just wait
For the day they are finally gone

Education

Written 29th July 2016
Drayton Manor Grammar School - Class of '72

Education really begins at home
As a baby learns to eat and drink
Some use a dummy and others not
Love play, sleep and start to think

Nursery school is the first outside experience
A chance to mingle at a very tender age
Learning the basics to begin the journey
Which will end when you earn your first wage

Infant's school can be an exciting time
Learning more and lots of play
Sometimes being noisy and laughing out loud
Such a pleasant way to spend the day

Junior school is the starter course
As we learn about discipline and rules
We have teachers for different subjects
And they won't suffer any fools

Grammar or high school is the main course
Where serious decisions have to be made
To pass our exams and do our very best
And achieve the highest grade

Those lucky enough to have their dessert
Will make it to university
Three years hard work will make it all worthwhile
And be proud to leave with a degree

Television

Written 13th June 2013
Published in Cover to Cover - A Collection of Poetry

What's the one thing we have in common, on our planet earth?
It is the television, though is it really worth
Spending so much time hypnotised by the set
Alone, with family, or snuggled up with our favourite pet?

When TV did first appear, it had so much mystery
It gave us new horizons, reminded us of history
We watched in awe, as more and more programmes were made
News, sport and the adverts, those memories never fade

Each had their favourite cartoon growing up as a child
Then the clowns and comedians appeared, and everybody smiled
There've been dramas, documentaries, so much variety
All tastes catered for, to satisfy you and me

It brought everything closer to home, even the monarchy
The Queen's various celebrations and any tragedy
Its influence has been so great, we believe everything we see
Though many living now, remember when there was only the BBC

And as we enter the 21st century, changes galore can be found
So much so it's a pity when we see an empty playground
Television certainly has its place in society
But no-one should be brainwashed thinking it's always reality

So don't be afraid to switch the set off, when you are at home
There are so many other things to do, so many places to roam
Talking, playing, reading, or listening to music too
Try never to let the television be the ruler of you

Music

Written 18th October 2012

If music be the food of love, play on
In time, everyone has their favourite song
There has always been a variety to bring us pleasure
And the talent involved you can never measure

Do you like rock, blues, reggae or pop?
House music, indie, jazz or hip-hop?
So many different styles, for us to enjoy
Listening or dancing with a girl or a boy

Then there is classical and opera too
Reach those highest notes and your face might turn blue
We sing and we hum to help the day pass
Our heads filled with music, whether it's slow or fast

We know our doh, ray, me, fah, soh, lah, te, doh
And love the music, whether the volume is high or low
It is played at all celebrations, from the moment we are born
For birthdays and weddings and the time that we mourn

So, clap your hands, whistle and sing when you can
Appreciate life's music, no matter from which land
All instruments make sounds in their own special way
They are with us forever, whether we can or cannot play

David Bowie (Part 1)

Written 14th January 2014
As featured in Immortal Idols

Can it really be a half century
Since the story of David Bowie began
He was born David Jones and his mind was set
To carry out and fulfill his plan

He always knew he would be a star
Changed his name to suit his style
The world of David Bowie, his very first album
Though it was always going to take him a while

Space Oddity followed, as man walked on the moon
And how psychedelic a track to applause
Ground Control to Major Tom
So, futuristic, appropriate, and without any flaws

He was innovative, his next work was pure rock
The Man Who Sold the World left you in a trance
With synthesisers, lyrics to make you think
He never left anything to chance

Hunky Dory was a delight for all
Changes for everyone and more
Loved the Kook's song, about his boy
Is there Life on Mars? No-one was sure

Then came the creation of Ziggy Stardust
An androgynous person who spoke of a Starman
He strutted his stuff, reaching out to us all
Were there really Five years left in God's plan?

Who will love Aladdin Sane, he asked
His face painted blue and red to shock
The Jean Genie lived on his back
And Time spoke of the ever-ticking clock

So many more albums made since those days
Changing image again and again
From the thin white duke to the recluse he became
So much going on in his brain

And one day we will all be heroes, as he told us
His music will be forgotten never
We were lucky to enjoy, such genius in our lives
His name will live on forever

(Part 2 - The Final Years)

In memory of David Bowie 08/01/47-10/01/16
Written 11th August 2016
As featured in Immortal Idols

David Bowie was always changing his style
And remained several steps ahead of the rest
Though it would always be hard for him to equal
His material up to 1974, his very best

However, he still had great success in between
That era and the end of the century
The Berlin Trilogy and Let's Dance album
He was the star of Live Aid for all to see

After pushing the boundaries even further
With the likes of albums Outside and Earthling
It was refreshing to return to ballads in Hours
And prove how well he could still sing

And so he entered the 21st century anew
With cracking albums Heathen and Reality
A fast beat to both and showing the world
The talent remained, and how lucky were we

Little did we know his health deteriorated
And it took ten years for the next album to arrive
Though The Next Day was quite magnificent
And showed that he was very much alive

Sadly there was not long left to go
With his last masterpiece due for release
Blackstar his final epitaph
And now may the genius rest in peace

Christmas

Written 29th November 2012
Published in A Year Gone By - A Collection of Poetry

It's Christmas, a time for loved ones and family
For mistletoe and mulled wine, and the christmas tree
Children smiling and laughing, with excitement in their eyes
Hoping all their presents and their wishes, do materialise

Everyone has their own favourite part of the celebration
Of Jesus Christ's birth, we're together as a nation
It's such a lovely time of year, with lights shining so bright
And carol singers can be heard through the day and night

There is so much to eat and drink, and oh so much to do
Do you visit family or do they come to you?
It's the time of year for turkey, with roasties and the sprouts
Mince pies too and Christmas pud, as everybody shouts

Crackers pulled, some you win, and there are gifts galore
Don't drink too much, or before you know it, everyone will hear you snore
You play games and watch TV, and repeats are often shown
But spare a thought, for those not so fortunate, who spend Christmas alone

So, Merry Christmas to you all, wherever you may be
Let's hope our wishes do come true, for you and for me
Be kind and thoughtful, enjoy it all, starting with Christmas Eve
And always remember it is better to give than ever to receive

51

New Year
Written 3rd January 2014

New year, old year, which is better we ask?
New ideas, old ideas, are we ready for any task?
One year older, one year wiser, do we ever learn
From our mistakes? Some repeated, no matter which way we turn

Life is always full of mystery, new challenges every day
Walking, driving, working, sleeping, finding time to play
Sometimes silent, other times noisy, nothing stays the same
Laughing, crying, praying, complaining, bow our heads in shame

Aware good health is paramount and hope we can stay well
So many diseases all around, no-one can ever tell
Each day a birth, a wedding, a funeral, a smile or a tear
Wherever we are on our planet, we are never far from fear

Though best be positive, things can only get better is often said
Use our experiences to stay calm and keep a wise head
I wish all could prosper in this life, though sadly this can never be
Just hope any suffering or disasters pass by you and me

Spring

Written 16th December 2014
*Published in It's the Most Wonderful Time of the Year
- 30.04.15*

Spring is my favourite time of year
As I was born late March, a time of rain
Flowers start blooming at the winter's end
And the clocks go forward again

The Grand National is the first sporting event
Always a spectacle to enjoy
The Boat Race and the FA Cup Final too
I have great memories from when I was a boy

It's the start of the financial year
A reminder to save and not only spend
Plan ahead for the summer holidays
Visiting family or a friend

Easter is a time to celebrate
And remember just what it means
When Christ died for our sins and rose again
We are human beings and not machines

April showers are welcome for the land
Though no-one wants to get too wet
We can still have fun, whether indoors or out
Playing together or with our favourite pet

As the days get longer in the month of May
And sunshine appears more often than not
It's a perfect time for a holiday
As the climate is never too cold or too hot

Yes, Spring is all things positive to me
And puts a smile upon my face
'Hope springs eternal' is the well known phrase
And the world can be a happy place

The Russian Winter

Written 19th February 2016 when on holiday
in the snow-clad Ural Mountains
Published in Poetic Forms 31.08.16

The Russian winter is unforgettable
With the land a carpet of snow
Temperatures can be as low as minus forty
Be sure to dress warm wherever you go

Driving long distances is possible
As all main roads are cleared using grit
You see rivers and lakes frozen over
As the sun melts snow on trees bit by bit

Much of the scenery really is spectacular
If you travel far and wide
Forests, mountains and waterfalls
Children playing on countless ice-slides

You will see much wildlife and nature
With dogs running in packs and cows on the roam
Riding on horse-back brings much pleasure
Though you appreciate the warmth when you are home

Life goes on as people still shop and chat
In the towns and villages too
Though if you don't understand the language
You are limited in what you can do

The cuisine is more varied than expected
Hot soup is welcome after skiing or being outside
It is certainly a land of intrigue and great history
Be it in Moscow, St Petersburg or anywhere the Russians have pride

Our Summer Holiday in Russia
Written 9th August 2014

Our summer holiday in Russia to see our grand-papa
We travelled from London, by plane, train and car
He lives a few hours from Perm, in the Ural Mountains so high
With forest trees so tall, they almost touch the sky

The sun was scorching so much when it shone
Though clouds would appear and then they were gone
The breeze was a relief, though the constant insects were not
They were there in abundance as it was so hot

Granddad grows such variety in his enormous garden
With a greenhouse, potatoes and every berry that you can imagine
We picked them any time of day, enjoying the sumptuous taste
With all the family to feed, none went to waste

Mother did the cooking of the local delicacies galore
Meat or fish with home-grown salad, always filling for sure
The house in Alexandrovsk was certainly in the most salubrious part
Each home had its own watchdog, never long for the barking to start

Once one dog started then others joined in too
Though they were all tied by a leash, yet if only we knew
That one house had new inhabitants, hadn't tied their dog so secure
As I walked with my daughter and her cousin, ran towards us, upset for sure

The cousin screamed, terrified, as it jumped on her first
With the owner suddenly appearing, fearing the worst
It circled around us, eyes fixed and barking so loud
We huddled together in our small nervous crowd

Would you believe it, we were all bitten on our leg
As the owner felt our horror, tried in vain to beg
Her excitable dog to not attack any more
Before finally catching it and closing its jaw

An ambulance was called as soon as we returned home
Everyone was shocked the dog had been free to roam
We were taken to hospital and antiseptic given to prevent infection
While I was given a precautionary tetanus injection

The police were quick to arrive and make a full report
And established immediately who was at fault
Though punishment always takes plenty of time
With all the necessary paperwork, despite the obvious crime

We tried to enjoy the rest of our stay
Most of it spent in the garden and play
Badminton, volleyball, and hide and seek too
Indoors it was chess, cards and always something to do

Granddad loved going fishing with his son
Having done that before not my idea of fun
Though one day they caught at least twenty fish
Clearly surpassing any fisherman's wish

And so the summer holiday came to its end
It had been eventful, including dinner with a neighbouring friend
As we hugged each other and said our goodbyes
Until we next meet, and we know how time flies

Trans-Siberian Express

Written 6th August 2014

Oh to be lucky and ride on the Trans-Siberian Express
With the mileage that it covers you can only guess
The experience we had, we can never forget
As the train departed Moscow and the sun already set

First class was the only way to enjoy it at its best
But even then it wouldn't be easy to have enough rest
Twenty hours on the train rattling at speed
Could spend time enjoying the views, eat, sleep or read

There was supposed to be TV and internet access too
However, neither were connected, had to find other things to do
The never-ending forest with different shades of green
And lakes of different sizes were everywhere to be seen

As we passed through nameless stations in the blink of an eye
We felt so close to nature, who would really want to fly?
Coloured houses of different shapes, so silent night and day
People up at the crack of dawn, merrily on their way

An eerie silence only broken, by the sound of our noisy train
The weather ever-changing, burning sun, mist and rain
Sometimes two trains passing, close enough to almost touch
Conversation heard in Russian, though didn't understand much

We noticed the odd high-rise building with windows broken too
Suddenly it's clear for miles, with an uninterrupted view
We wonder what mysteries lie in the forest, with the trees growing so tall
As horses and dogs are seen running, listening to their owners call

Out of the blue a queue of traffic, waiting for the train to pass by
As our journey continues, with an ever-changing sky
Then for no reason we slow down, almost to a tortoise pace
No-one knows why, as there is no communication in place

Finally we pick up speed and know that the next stop is ours
Have we really been on the same train for over 20 hours?
The relief as we pull into Perm, our destination
While others stay on the train, until they reach their station

Would we take the ride again, probably not as once is enough
Even though we were in first class and not sleeping rough
So, if you get the chance, you too can get to know
The Trans-Siberian Express adventure, with so far to go

Snow

Written 18th November 2013
Published in In Other Words - A Collection of Poetry

One of life's mysteries, it certainly remains
Whenever frost appears, icing as it rains
Then suddenly we feel the coolness in the air
Snow is upon us and landing everywhere

Before we even know it, there is a carpet of white
Children love to see it, play in it and fight
Throwing snowballs at each other, laughing when it lands
On any face or body, without a care for their cold hands

To many of us it's a nuisance, something we can do without
You have to tread so very carefully, if you are out and about
And temperatures are freezing, how can it be so cold?
Spare a thought for the less mobile, especially the old

Sometimes it seems to stay forever, will it ever melt?
When you touch it, the strangest sensation you have ever felt
Though building snowmen of different sizes really can be fun
It's sad when they're no longer with us, because of the burning sun

So whether or not you wish to see it, when our winter's here
You can be certain many tourists, suddenly appear
Some have never seen it, in their homelands oh so warm
Just hope you're never stranded in a serious snow storm

The Four Seasons
Written 5th April 2016

Sparkling
Pretty
Refreshing
Inspiring
Nurturing
Glorious

Sunny
Ubiquitous
Mesmerising
Memorable
Enthralling
Radiant

Apprehensive
Unexpected
Transitional
Unforgiving
Melancholy
Noticeable

Wintry
Icy
Nocturnal
Torrid
Endemic
Relentless

Travel
Written 2nd November 2012

What an amazing place, our planet earth
With so many wonders to see
Every country has something worth
Be it views or history

Just think so very long ago
When mankind was starting to learn
How to move to and fro
Seeking new places to turn

At first, we could only go by foot
Then horses came to the rescue
As less people decided to just stay put
And searched for somewhere new

As time moved on and other ways were found
To explore and learn more of our world
It became far easier to get around
As every lands flag was unfurled

The boat, the car, the train, the plane
Each serving our purpose to enjoy
Meeting more people, we're not the same
Whether we are a girl or a boy

And who knows what the future will bring
As we travel from place to place
New inventions are in the offing
As we reach into outer space

Where Would You Rather Be?
Written 7th April 2016

Would you rather be in England
Where the land is oh so green
Scotland, Wales or Ireland too
And the islands around and between

Or would you prefer continental Europe
France, Germany, Italy or Greece
Perhaps Spain, Portugal or an island in the Med
Scandinavia might be cold if you please

Would you rather be in the USA
With over fifty states to choose?
As west as California or as east as Florida
A country that's always in the news

How about Australia or New Zealand
Or are they really too far away?
Maybe the mystery of Russia, Asia and the Far East
Though would you understand what they say?

The Middle East or Africa are surely far too hot
Where the scorching sun is there to stay
And the islands of the Atlantic or Pacific
Far from the hustle and bustle of life everyday

Our planet has so much variety and it really is fate
As to where we are born and what we'll see
But if you really had the choice to decide
Where would you rather be?

The Greeks

Written 17th December 2015

The Greeks have always been a proud race
Athens and Sparta's reputations well-known
Thousands of years and the Acropolis remains in place
With its marble and original stone

Homer wrote so many stories of heroes of old
The Iliad and the Odyssey too
How Leonidas and his 300 Spartans were so bold
And the twelve labours that Hercules went through

Helen's was the face which launched a thousand ships
As Achilles slew Hector of Troy
The wooden horse gift then the sound of swords and whips
And the Greeks had their victory and joy

In philosophy there are so many to name
Plato, Aristotle and Socrates to begin
Pythagoras and Archimedes made their claim
In mathematics, science and debating

Zeus was the king of the gods long ago
With Hera always close by his side
The mortals worshipped them and revered them so
And their enemies had nowhere to hide

Alexander the Great was the most famous of all
As he built the great empire during his reign
He travelled far and wide before a fever saw him fall
And Greece would never have the same power again

So many nations learnt from the Greek way of life
And the Romans were the very first
Though abuse and corruption remained rife
And many slaves died of hunger and thirst

Many centuries have since come and gone
The Spartan motto is always "never say die"
The Greeks brought civilisation, knowledge, games and song
I'm proud to be an Evzona and hold my head high

Cyprus

Written 19th April 2016
Photo: My grandfather
- holding the national flag in WWII

Three hundred and forty days sunshine a year
Cyprus, a paradise island in the Med
The people are friendly and love to entertain
And many couples go there to be wed

The sky so blue and the sea so serene
And there are water sports galore
You can play tennis, golf or even go-kart
Dance to the bouzouki, no island offers you more

Cypriot cuisine is superb and varied
To try a fish or meat meze is a must
So many starters, main courses with Greek salad
And a freshness you can certainly trust

You really can shop until you drop
Buying various produce to enjoy at your leisure
Whether leather goods or a plethora of delicacies
Haggling with the locals is always a pleasure

Rent a car and travel far and wide
There is spectacular scenery all around
Drive along the coast or high up in the mountains
Breath-taking glorious views to be found

Remember sun-glasses, sun-hat and sun-factor cream
You will need them all for sure
And once you've experienced the magic of Cyprus
You will want to return for more

The Greek Meze

Written 5th August 2016
First published in The Great British Write off - Power of the Pen 31.12.16

The Greek Meze is a most sumptious feast
Which will fill any appetite
Starter dips taramasalata, tzatziki and houmus
With hot pitta bread as you enjoy each bite

Halloumi cheese with lunza bacon
Garlic mushrooms and spicy sausage
Well-presented dishes come one by one
Waiters careful to avoid any damage

An array of fish will come your way
Kalamari, whitebait and cuttlefish too
Red mullet or sea-bream freshly caught
From the Mediterranean Sea so blue

Spinach in pastry and stuffed vine leaves
Filled with tasty mince and rice
Healthy Greek salad and feta cheese
Yes it really is that nice

Kebabs of chicken, lamb or pork
Their appealing aroma lingers on
Kleftiko, stifado or afelia to enjoy
Don't rush and you'll have no indigestion

Don't forget to choose your favourite wine
St Panteleimon for me and water is ok
When you've tried it once you'll want it again
You'll never tire of the Greek Meze

Olympics
Written 3rd August 2016

Outstanding achievement to take part
Loyal to their country and all heart
Yearning to do their very best
Motivation to beat all the rest
Performing to an audience worldwide
Individuals or teams taking pride
Competitive to win a medal at least
Sporting glory and a memorable feast

If We Could Go Back
Written 5th September 2016

If we really could go back in time
Would we have done anything differently?
Some matters were always out of our hands
Though there were always choices for you and me

Do you wish you had been born in a different country
Or at a different time or in a different family?
If you grew up poor do you wish you grew up rich
And maybe live amongst the most wealthy?

If you are male do you wish you had been female
And if you are female do you wish you were a male?
Or some might wish they had been something in between
Though therein lies another tale

Do you wish that you weren't bullied
Or weren't known as the playground bully?
Do you wish you'd learnt more at school
And reached your potential more fully?

Do you wish you had stayed single or married?
Or maybe you married far too young
Wish you had never been through a divorce
Had children and been financially stung

Did you suffer physical and mental abuse
From strangers or members of your family?
Prevention was always better than a cure
Then maybe you would have lived more happily

Do you wish you had tried much harder
To make your childhood dreams come true
To be a sports star, singer or actor
Or actually do what you always wanted to?

Do you wish you had chosen a different career
Or been promoted to reward your expertise and commitment?
Do you feel that you let yourself down
Or others did when it was never their intent?

Do you wish you hadn't drunk, smoked or gambled
And would have lived life squeaky clean?
Would you have always told the truth
Or used language that wasn't so obscene?

There are so many things we would have changed
Though hindsight is a powerful tool indeed
Fate and circumstances have always played their part
With many having more and others far less than they need

Tender Loving Care Trilogy
Written 1st August 2016

Tender
Emotional
Natural
Delicate
Erotic
Romantic

Loving
Obedient
Voluptuous
Irresistible
Nubile
Gentle

Careful
Amiable
Reliable
Equal

Capitalism, Socialism and Idealism Trilogy

Written 1st August 2016

Control
Accumulate
Profit
Individual
Threatening
Advantage
Luxury
Imposing
Systematic
Money

Social
Organised
Challenging
Impatient
Authentic
Loyal
Indiscriminate
State
Money

Ideal
Democratic
Euphoric
Attainable
Leveller
Inspirational
Sharing
Money

Drinking, Smoking and Gambling
Written 27th September 2016

Drunk
Ridiculous
Irresponsible
Nuisance
Knackered
Inebriated
Nasty
Goggle-eyed

Smell
Miscarriage
Odour
Killer
Inhalation
Nauseating
Germs

Games
Addiction
Money
Bankrupt
Losing
Income
Nervous
Gaining

It Never Happened

Written 19th February 2015

God created the planets and stars
Dinosaurs walked the earth
Homo sapiens evolved slowly but surely
Learnt about food, shelter and survival

Mankind discovered how to make weapons
More importantly, how to use them
To keep alive when lives were in danger
They multiplied and formed different races

Spread around the earth, coping with the elements
Living in fear of invaders and predators
The strong abusing the weak, as rulers took power
Always wanting more, and not caring about those suffering

Some lives so short-lived, while others blossomed
As they valued life and became materialistic
Countries scared of each other, and wars inevitable
Through religion or just taking slaves and possessions

As centuries and millenniums came and went
Eventually bringing holocausts and nuclear bombs
Never any sight of an end to the cruelty
Yet they say it never happened

If Only

Written 25th September 2014

If only I was born with a silver spoon in my mouth, if only
I would have grown up all posh and everything done for me, if only
No worries about what I could or could not have, if only
A financial security for the rest of my life, if only

The other side of the coin is a nightmare, if only
To be born into poverty with a constant shortage of food and clothes, if only
To be jealous and resentful through no fault of my own, if only
To resort to stealing without shame to have what I want, if only

Then there is the happy or unhappy medium, if only
To be born with enough to get by but never totally satisfied, if only
To keep both feet on the ground as some climb the ladder and others fall down,
if only
To think what might have been and what fate awaits, if only

Who knows, I could have been born or become disabled, if only
Then life would be even harder to cope with, if only
Imagine being unable to see, hear or speak, if only
And being among the strongest and not the weak, if only

Turn the clock back to the very beginning of time, if only
How did it all start, was it creation or just a fluke, if only
It all began to go wrong when nations were formed, if only
And rather than a peaceful life here, we seek life elsewhere, if only

Where, When, Who, What, Why?

Written 20th April 2016

Where
Here
Everywhere
Rotating
Earth

When
Hour
Early
Never

Who
Human
Omnipresent

What
Hearsay
Actual
Transparent

Why
How
You

Life's a Roller Coaster
Written 29th September 2014

From beginning to end the race is on
Do we stop and think and ask why
A demanding baby, daughter or son
Who scream and shout and cry

We need attention and continuous care
As we face the everyday chores
There's hardly any time to spare
As we rush in and out of doors

From the moment we are first awake
The crazy chaos begins to show
Washing, brushing, breakfast to make
Blaming others for being slow

Children in school with so much to learn
Can't get it right always
Raising their arms and waiting their turn
Hoping for a teacher's praise

Going to work brings so much stress
Whether driving, taking the bus or a train
Surrounded by traffic, sometimes a mess
And everyone taking the strain

If we are late we feel so low
As others are into their stride
We must be positive, keep on the go
There's no place we can hide

Look around you during the day
And see the race never ends
Rushing at lunch time, no time to play
And little time to chat with your friends

As time ticks on and night draws nigh
Where did the day really go?
Soon it's tomorrow as we look to the sky
Life's a roller coaster, as we all know

The Internet
Written 30th September 2014

Where did the internet come from
And how did we survive before?
It's a necessary tool for all
Leaving us wanting more

It can answer every question
Well every question but one
How was the world created
And did God make the first human?

Many have turned their back on books
So they can surf the net
On social media sites like Facebook
And that's how people have met

It's a whole wide world out there
We must sort the fake from the real
Some waiting to take advantage
Be careful before you show how you feel

Then there is the worry of mind control
As some will impose their view
Trying to stir up hatred and war
Don't let them influence you

We must try and be positive where we can
And use the knowledge we gain
Research is good and plenty to learn
So much to retain in our brain

And as the 21st century rolls on
What will the future bring?
New inventions replacing the old
We can still never know everything

Let's hope the internet can stay a friend
And never let us down
We need its support in all walks of life
As the world goes around and around

Work

Written 2nd October 2012

If you work you get paid, and if you don't you won't
There are some who have it made, there are many who don't

The more you learn the more you earn, unless you have a skill
Life is full of twists and turns, an uncertainty and a thrill

You can still enjoy yourself at work, making friends anew
Be committed and never shirk, they can rely on you

Job satisfaction is a must, to help you through the day
Be confident and build a trust, be sure of what you say

If things go wrong try and remain strong, you can always turn it round
Always smile and go the extra mile, and you'll be on solid ground

Every day brings something new, to challenge your mind too
Rise and shine then all will be fine, remember we work our whole life through

British Airways

Written 20th December 2016 in
memory of my service there from
30th May 1978 – 31st October 1990

British Airways, our national carrier
Of red, white and blue
In the 1970s our slogan was
'We'll take more care of you'

We have always flown to more places
Than any other airline worldwide
Our reputation for being the world's favourite
With a service full of pride

Our flagship was supersonic Concorde
Which was faster than the speed of sound
It was sad that unfortunate events
Mean it's no longer around

Our staff are multi-national
Always confident and a welcoming smile
Our cabins provide their amenities
Wherever you travel, for every mile

Our fleet now includes the Dreamliner
Which is the largest aircraft we have known
We look forward to you flying with us
With our cabin crew, you are never alone

The Latymerian

Written 2nd October 2013 in appreciation of my daughter,
Alexandra, the Walter Legge music scholar
Published in Forward Poetry - Poetry in Motion

The Latymerian is so proud
And goes to school to learn
A boy or girl stands out in the crowd
With energy to burn

No two days are the same
There's so much variety
Whether studying hard or playing a game
The determination is there to see

The head inspires his staff so well
Their knowledge and enthusiasm thrives
From the morning arrival 'til the sound of the bell
As the pupils get on with their lives

At lunch-time they are spoilt for choice
With cuisine from far and wide
Some fit in homework, away from the noise
While others just play outside

The history is there for all to see
So many famous have been here before
Actors, musicians, stars of sport and TV
And we know there will be many more

The time spent at the school
Will never be forgotten for sure
Each finds their own way, and follows the rule
A Latymerian for evermore

85

London
Written 3rd March 2016

It's the greatest city in the world
With a history all so unique
Over eight million live here and many commute
Every single day of the week

It is home to the Queen and most wealthy
Properties worth millions in Park Lane and Mayfair
Shops such as Harrods, and Fortnum and Mason
And people crowd the streets everywhere

Landmarks aplenty, where to begin
St Paul's, Tower Bridge and Big Ben
Westminster Abbey, Houses of Parliament, Buckingham Palace
And many tourist attractions always open

Ride on the London Eye or the Emirates Cable Car
Visit Canary Wharf and the Shard
In April the London Marathon takes place
The sound of feet pounding the streets hard

There's the Lord Mayor's show and Notting Hill Carnival
And the changing of the guard every day
See the pigeons in Trafalgar Square
Or watch the joggers in Hyde Park make their way

So many visitors come from far and wide
London has so much to see and do
The open-top bus ride and River Thames cruise
Olympic Stadium, Wimbledon and Wembley too

Maybe it's because I'm a Londoner
That I love London town
It is a much changed capital these past fifty years
Though remains the jewel in our crown

The London Underground
Written 31st December 2015

Tens of thousands of people every day
Using the London Underground
We start our journey at any time
And at every station can be found

The rush hour is everyone's nightmare
As we queue for tickets or wait for a train
Hoping we won't be late for work
The whole process is taxing on the brain

They seem so crowded the trains are packed
As the majority try to grab a seat
Some have long journeys, others short
Everyone is quick on their feet

The trains seem more modern nowadays
Yet still there can be a delay
Signal failures, defective trains, a passenger taken ill
Just hope it doesn't happen today

We take the speed of travel for granted
As the trains go to and fro
Though whenever there is a tube strike
We suffer so much, as we know

People are generally caring
Respecting the signs at the end seats planned
To allow expectant mothers and the elderly
A less painful journey and not have to stand

Everyone with their own method of passing the time
Having a quick nap, reading a paper or book
Texting, playing games or listening to music
Or merely sitting with a blank look

It's been with us for over a hundred years
And each year is used more and more
The saddest of all are those who take their own lives
While seven/seven etched in our hearts for evermore

Wimbledon

Written 6th July 2015 in memory of being Greenford Boys
Singles and Doubles Tennis Champion 1970 and 1971

Wimbledon has always been special to me
Though I have never seen a match live
Grew up watching it on TV
And started playing myself at the age of five

Rod Laver was a boyhood hero of mine
An Australian left-hander, so natural
His serve and volley was always so fine
His shots so effective for someone not tall

He encouraged me to do well in my youth
As I tried hard to copy his style
He dominated for ten years that is the truth
And my winning four trophies made it worthwhile

My favourite girl was Margaret Court
As she moved around so athletic and graceful
Her matches with Billie Jean King so hard fought
And the margins between them so very small

Then we were graced by the ice cool Swede
Bjorn Borg was his name
Unusual with a double-handed backhand at speed
He totally changed the game

His fierce rival was John McEnroe
An American with determination and attitude
His feelings he was never afraid to show
Though some found them aggressive and rude

Then Germany produced two amazing stars
Boris Becker and Steffi Graf
They were young and fresh and raised the bars
Boris falling so often making us laugh

Martina Navratilova ruled for so many years
Effective all over the court
As she broke records and was reduced to tears
And became another great for the sport

The power game then came into play
As more Americans ruled the roost
Pete Sampras winning non-stop along the way
Giving hard-hitters a boost

But then out of the blue came someone new
Roger Federer, a touch player so serene
He was my new hero as opponents struggled to
Cope with his shots precise and clean

His dominance had not been witnessed before
As he won more grand slams than them all
And he may have won so many more
Had Nadal and Djokovic not come to the ball

These three legends were then joined by a Brit
As Andy Murray became the first to win
Since Fred Perry in 1936 it is writ
And the partisan crowd made a din

We've had British ladies champions not so long ago
Anne Jones and Virginia Wade too
Serena Williams now dominates as we know
Wimbledon's excitement will always shine through

Chess

Written 19th February 2016 in memory of
being Drayton Manor Grammar School
6th form Chess Champion in 1973

Chess is such a power game
Which can be a struggle for all
Played by the old and the young
And by the big and the small

Will you play as white
Or will you play as black
Will you need to defend
Or will you want to attack

The queen certainly is the most
Dangerous piece on the board
She moves around at will
And no mistake can you afford

The rook moves as her main support
Forwards, backwards, sideways in a line
While you may even need to castle
With the king some of the time

The bishops and knights have their own agenda
Used wisely they can have their say
And even the pawns which seem so inferior
Can often have their role to play

A game can seem to take an eternity
Though some may be as quick as a speed-date
The moment of truth is finally reached
Your king is helpless when it is checkmate

Be Your Valentine

Written 14th February 2015
Published in *Love is in the air*
Volume Two - 30.09.15

In a world in which we live in
With so much animosity
Isn't it refreshing when fate
Brings two people close in harmony

The excitement so heart-felt
When you first make contact
As the emotions come together
You can't fight them that's a fact

A first kiss so memorable
And something to enjoy
Holding hands, embracing
Such passion between girl and boy

I believe in the age of chivalry
Though for many it seems to have past
Why should a first meeting
End up being the last

As you learn more about each other
Every day discovering something new
Your love begins to grow
And your feelings are so true

The way to a girl's heart
Is with tenderness, love and care
Chocolates and flowers are welcome
Though more important to always be there

Be happy if you are lucky to find
Someone precious and oh so fine
Treat them as you wish to be treated
They'll be your valentine

The Very Far Distant Future
Written 16th December 2015

Can you imagine the thought of the year 5015?
Indeed a time three thousand years from now
What good and bad may happen in between
And will mankind continue to survive somehow?

The Sphinx in Egypt is almost five thousand years old
I wonder what will still be standing so far ahead
How temperatures may fluctuate from hot and cold
And will people still remember those of us long dead

Maybe space travel will be common-place
And humans will no longer have ethnic identities
Will life still be such a crazy rat race
Or will we just come and go as we please?

We could all be micro-chipped from birth
And immunised to keep us disease-free
Everyone might understand life's precious worth
Living for much longer and more healthily

I wonder just how humans will look
And what we will drink and eat
Will there still be such a thing as a book
And will some animals still be used as meat?

Our imagination can run wild at the thought
Of robots to be seen everywhere
Will humans still work and play sport?
Could life possibly be more fair?

Will there be such a thing as a family
Or will we merely just reproduce?
Can you imagine the 5015 versions of you and me?
Will people still be free to choose?

What buildings and landscapes will still remain
As time moves swiftly on and on?
Will we still travel by aeroplane
Or will new discoveries mean that is long gone?

It is a fascination for all I'm sure
We know we are determined to survive
Let's hope the future will see no rich or poor
And civilisation continues to thrive

Positive Horoscopes
Written 7th October 2016

Assertive
Responsible
Inspirational
Energetic
Sensual

Trustworthy
Approachable
Understanding
Reliable
Unique
Sensitive

Generous
Emotional
Mysterious
Inquisitive
Nostalgic
Intellectual

Caring
Adaptable
Nurturing
Calm
Emotional
Reassuring

Loyal
Enthusiastic
Optimistic

Virtuous
Intelligent
Responsible
Graceful
Organised

Loving
Idealist
Balanced
Reliable
Adaptable

Secretive
Commanding
Organised
Romantic
Passionate
Intense
Outgoing

Sincere
Adventurous
Generous
Intelligent
Truthful
Thoughtful
Active
Reliable
Independent
Understanding
Sociable

Caring
Ambitious
Practical
Responsible
Influential
Cautious
Optimistic
Reliable
Neat

Adventurous
Questioning
Unbiased
Amiable
Responsible
Independent
Understanding
Sincere

Peace-loving
Intuitive
Sensitive
Creative
Emotional
Sympathetic

The Planets and the Stars
Written 7th August 2013

When you gaze up at the sky, everything seems so afar
Especially at night, with the moon and shining star
They sometimes appear surreal, as you watch them come and go
One second they're there, the next they're gone, as clouds move to and fro

Time and time again, you'll hear the very same question
'Is there Life on Mars?' will always get a mention
It's as though we're desperate to find solace, that we are not alone
In the universe of planets and stars, some not always shown

They say women are from Venus, men from Mars, but is it really true?
Are women hot and men just cold? They must be kidding you
Our scientists searching every day, for the next discovery
Hoping to sight authentic UFOs, in the sky, on land or sea

Jupiter is all so cold and massive too, others must envy its size
Whilst Saturn and its unique rings, a wonder for our eyes
Neptune and Uranus both mystical, uninhabitable too
And Mercury so small, closest to the sun where temperatures grew

And here we are on Mother Earth, our home since time begun
We've seen it all, the good, the bad, the hardships and the fun
So the question asked, if we're looking up, is anyone looking down?
The mystery remains with us, whether we smile or frown

Drones

Written 11th August 2016

Delivering
Roaming
Observing
Nuisance
Endless
Spyware

The Sky

Written 12th August 2016

The sky is a fascination and always has been
Has it changed at all since time began?
Birds always roaming and clouds coming and going
It remains an ongoing mystery to man

Sometimes so serene with not a cloud in sight
A beautiful azure blue so pleasant on the eye
Though dark clouds mean that rain is not far away
No matter the weather, aeroplanes always fly

Spectacular scenery can emerge with red sky at night
And a full or double rainbow, a sight to behold
The seasons affect the sky sometimes so extreme
When it is boiling hot or freezing cold

When you look up high do you ever stop and think
How earth must look from any shining star
The sun and moon so bright at different times
And our planet looks so small from afar

Mad

Written 2nd March 2016

Obsession, despair, insane
Steam-rolling everything and anyone
Hell-bent on causing mayhem
Everyone suffers and no fun

On a mission to self-destruction
Using any means available to destroy
No morals or feelings just pain
To inflict on any girl or boy

How can anyone become so evil
Lose their mind and just run amok?
Anger-management is lost on them
It's everyday and no longer a shock

Some may have their own reasons
Never been taught right or wrong
No-one cared or maybe that's just an excuse
And they were just mad all along

Who's Complaining?
Written 20th July 2016

The weather is too hot and unbearable
But who's complaining?
We can't sleep at night and the heat is stifling
But would you prefer it to be raining?

To see the girls in their short summer dresses
Every full-blooded male's delight
Some so short they could spark a cardiac arrest
Others wearing shorts, oh so tight

Luckily in England it is not so hot too often
Otherwise we would find it hard to cope
Spare a thought for those lands with incessant heat
Where a much-needed breeze has little hope

Then when the weather changes as the sun disappears
And the blue sky becomes cloudy and grey
You can't please everyone so who's complaining
If it starts to rain all day?

We are fortunate to have four seasons to experience
With the very best and worst of the weather
Cold or hot or anything in between
It's just not worth complaining forever

Telling a Lie
Written 21st July 2016

Is there any time when anyone can tell a lie
To avoid the trauma that may follow?
Does anyone know the reason why
People might cause so much sorrow?

Being economical with the truth
Is a phrase we hear all the time
Better to remain silent and keep the peace
Or deny if accused of being a slime

Everyday someone regrets what they've done
If it means someone else has suffered and cried
Anger and violence is certainly no-one's idea of fun
Though the guilty must wish they never lied

It happens to families, friends and politicians too
It has become part of human nature we know
We can argue until we all turn blue
Time is the healer though that may be very slow

Boredom

Written 3rd November 2014
Published in Life's Prism
- A Collection of Poetry - 31.03.15

Sometimes we'll let out a yawn
And there are many reasons why
We start to yawn from when we are born
And continue until the day we die

Though what is it that makes us stretch away
Is it due to lack of sleep?
We can yawn whether working or at play
Our eyes feeling very deep

And if we attend a seminar or speech
At times our boredom will show
No matter what they are trying to teach
Do we really want to know?

Boredom can set in at any time
It's so easy just to slip away
Life is precious until our very last chime
We should appreciate it night and day

Does It Matter?
Written 26th April 2016

Vote for a leader, vote for a captain
Whoever invented the vote?
Hands shown or ballot papers counted
Some winners may stand and gloat

Do we ask ourselves, if it is fair
Or is there corruption sometimes afoot?
Can every vote really make a difference
Or do most people not give a hoot?

Vote for me they say, as they try to win
And prove themselves the best
But when elected and having the power
Do they honestly care about the rest?

Confusion reigns, as no-one really knows
What the future may hold
Does it really matter, who wins each time
Whether we are young, maturing or old?

Brexit

Written 20th July 2016
Published in Political Fortunes - 21.04.17

Decision day, 23rd June, came and went
Would we remain in Europe or would we leave
The politicians worked us all to and fro
We just didn't know who to believe

The aftermath still isn't clear
Will our population start to decrease?
So many different nationalities living here
Can we live side by side in peace?

The early signs are not so good
With race crimes reported almost every day
Some looking for an excuse to make matters worse
Immigrants wondering whether they should leave or stay

The next few years really will be key
And our country will learn our fate
Let's hope we prosper and maintain respect
Our citizens living together without any hate

Invisible

Written 29th October 2012

Immortal, invisible God only wise
Do we see what is in front of us, or are we just surprised?
Some say they know it all, though pride comes before a fall
Whilst others who may know nothing, can still learn to walk tall

Life can be a vacuum, and an everyday maze
Whether we're faced with torrential rain, or the sun's hot rays
Which way to turn, do we go straight, left or right?
Do we touch or smell, or only use our sight?

Each of us merely trying to find, a meaning to it all
Why are some fat or thin, others tall or small?
Some may listen, others not, quite invisible
Each page turning in our book, until our final call

The First Few Hours
and the Last Few Hours
Written 9th October 2016

Does anyone remember the first few hours?
Where am I? Who am I?
What am I, a girl or a boy?
How did I arrive, and did I fall from the sky?

I can't see, but I can hear
Am I in hospital or in a house?
Am I normal or have any defects
And maybe I am somewhere else

Do I have two parents or only one?
Am I the first or do I have a sibling?
Have I been born into a rich household or poor?
Will I be deprived or have everything?

There is no turning back now
I cry and may even scream
No matter, I am here to stay
Life is precious and not just a dream

Where are we for the last few hours?
Are we in a caring nursing home?
Maybe we are at home with family
Or are we just waiting all alone?

Wherever we are, we could be reflecting
Did we have a happy life or sad?
Were we good, kind and, honest as could be
Or were we selfish and sometimes nasty or bad?

Maybe we have no choice for our finale
Could be in a war-zone or in extreme weather danger
Suffering with a terminal illness or a sudden heart-attack
Are we staring into space or with a friend or a stranger?

This comes to us all, no matter who we are
The butcher, the baker and the candlestick-maker
The memories linger on and we hope we do not suffer
No-one wants to be in pain, before they meet their maker

LAUGH

A Trip Down Comedy Lane

Written 20th February 2015

It all started in black and white
Buster Keaton and Charlie Chaplin the first
To make us laugh ourselves silly
Until we were ready to burst

Then came Laurel and Hardy
A crazier pair you would never meet
"That's another fine mess you got me into"
Fat Oli said as you fell off your seat

The Marx brothers always entertained
With a variety of jokes and song
Groucho with moustache and eyes gleaming
And his brothers just tagging along

Bob Hope and Bing Crosby brought many smiles
In their endless films on the road
Slapstick humour at its best
And their one liners certainly flowed

Phil Silvers as Sergeant Bilko
Always looking to play a scam
Though no matter what he tried
Nothing ever went to plan

The Goons were ahead of their time
With scripts to make you roar
So much nonsense and voices changed
Peter, Spike, Harry and Michael were the four

Sellers was a master of disguise
And was perfect as Inspector Clouseau
How we laughed as he suffered each time
Cato attacked him and carnage would flow

Hancock was a pure genius
With his regular deadpan face
Sid James as his stooge to be abused
And certainly knew his place

The Carry On films were quite absurd
And so many stars were born
Chaos followed them all around
And their jokes were never worn

Then came gangly Tommy Cooper
With his fez instead of a hat
Pure comedy and magic together
And his famous phrase 'just like that'

Peter Cook and Dudley Moore jousting
Always trying to have the last word
Though it was hard for either not to laugh
As their sketches were just so absurd

Morecambe and Wise were well suited
With guests ridiculed all the time
By their continuous mischievous gags
And their parting 'bring me sunshine'

The Two Ronnies were just as funny
Dressing up and larking around
Such memorable faces whenever necessary
Taking turns to be the clown

Dave Allen had the driest humour
When sitting there in his chair
He pushed the boundaries further and further
Humouring religion when others wouldn't dare

The Monty Python gang were most unusual
With sketches never seen before
"And now for something completely different"
So zany and leaving us wanting more

Fawlty Towers was the funniest sit-com
Every episode, madness all the way through
As Basil strutted his stuff each week
Sybil, Polly, Manuel and guests too

Not the Nine O'clock News changed direction
Making a mockery of everything topical
Rowan, Mel, Griff and Pamela all
Combining perfectly and ever so comical

Billy Connolly was surely a strange yin
Often swearing the air blue
Loud, emotional and even singing a song
Though a lot of what he said was true

More recently there's been Jack Dee, Lee Evans
Michael McIntyre and others too
I'm sorry if I've not mentioned some favourites
May laughter continue to please me and you

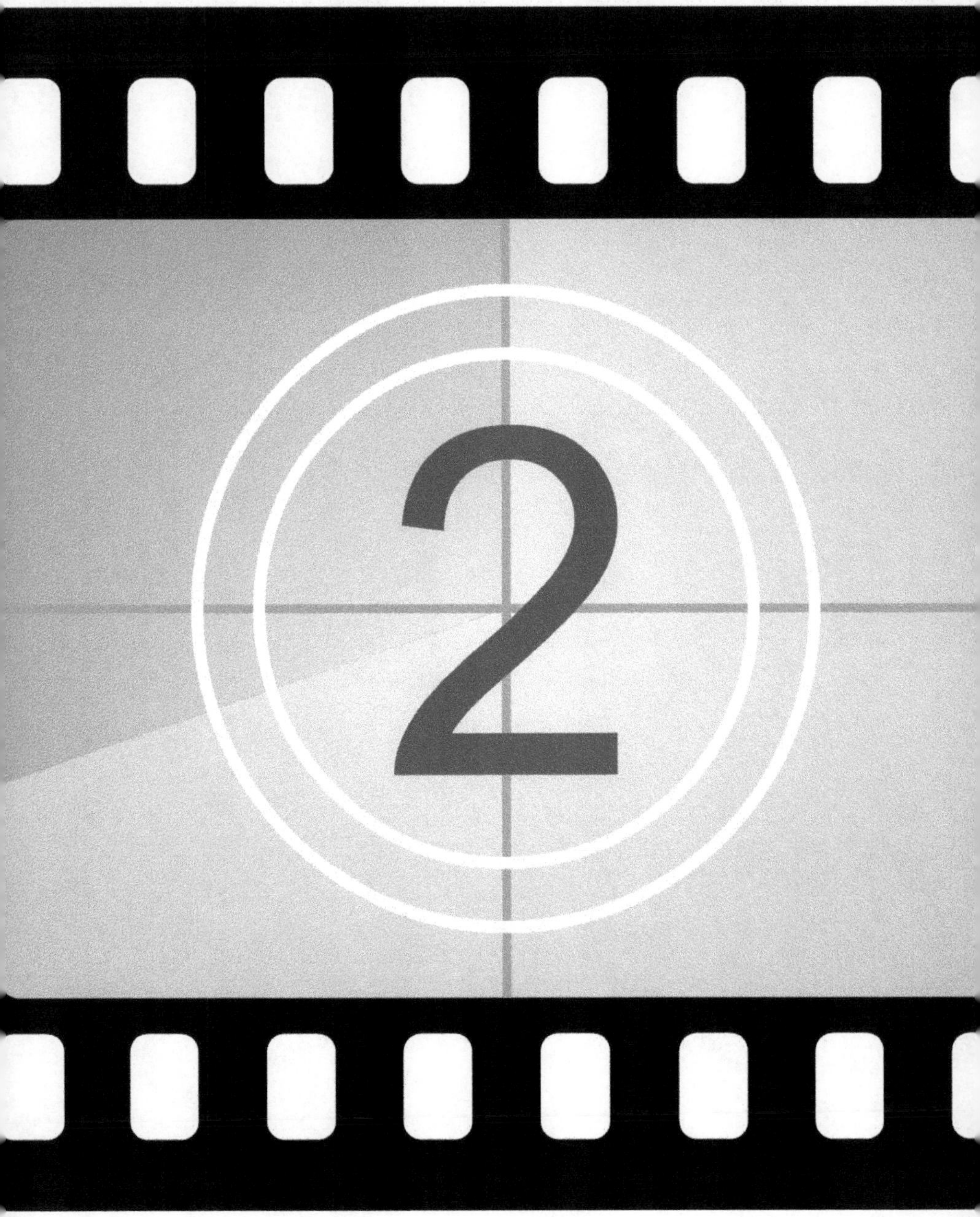
2

A Trip Back to the Old Great Movies
Written 18th November 2015

Everyone has their favourite movies
They may watch again and again
Some you may not have seen for ages
Then they return like a long lost friend

My first was the Wizard of Oz
A wonderful journey for a child
Then Snow White and the Seven Dwarfs
And the Jungle Book which was funny and wild

Gone with the Wind was the first romance
And Casablanca followed in its wake
Then the passion that was Dr Zhivago
And Love Story with so much heartbreak

"I'm Spartacus, I'm Spartacus" they cried
Ben Hur and the Big Country knew no bounds
While the Magnificent Seven and Zulu were glorious
And the war movies started their rounds

The spaghetti westerns were gripping but humorous too
An epic Once Upon a Time in the West
John Wayne winning everything singled handed
Though Clint Eastwood was always the best

Alfred Hitchcock was the master of suspense
We remember the shower scene in Psycho
Strangers on a Train, the Birds and North by North West
Rear Window and the scary Vertigo

So many wonderful musicals to enjoy
South Pacific, My Fair Lady and Carousel
The Sound of Music, Oliver and the ironic Cabaret
And the Fiddler on the Roof as well

We laughed ourselves silly at It's a Mad, Mad, Mad World
The Pink Panther movies always such fun
Those Magnificent Men in Their Flying Machines
And the madness of Monty Python

The Godfather was the first to have different parts
As it seemed to run for hours on end
Then Superman, Rocky and others did the same
The start of a never-ending trend

Stanley Kubrick was the best director of all
A Clockwork Orange fully broke new ground
Dr Strangelove, The Shining and Full Metal Jacket
2001: A Space Odyssey left us all spellbound

Steven Spielberg followed not far behind
With Close Encounters of the Third Kind and E.T.
Other sci-fis to make us jump like Alien and the Thing
Blade Runner most realistic you'll agree

The prison movies led by The Great Escape
And the greatest for me Papillon
Midnight Express and Escape from Alcatraz
The Green Mile and Shawshank Redemption

Emotions run high and tears to be found
In Sophie's Choice and Schindler's List
The agony and fear as everyone cried
Watching the life of the Pianist

And the great sport movies about our heroes
From World Cups and Olympics to inspire
I loved Ali, Champions and Grand Prix
And the determination in Chariots of Fire

I hope you've enjoyed my personal journey
Which started so very long ago
Cinema has always been powerful
We're engrossed even more than we know

Sheffield Wednesday

Written 4th December 2013
As featured in Forward Poetry "An Ode To..."

Since I was a small boy, there was only one team
And being champions or winning the cup was always my dream
Even though I was born in London's West
I chose Sheffield Wednesday above all the rest

I quickly learnt they played in colours blue and white
And I never will forget my very first sight
Of the magical stadium known as Hillsborough
That January day in 1970 with my older brother

The atmosphere was electric, there was so much noise
As we cheered them on in the cup, with the other girls and boys
We managed to beat West Brom by two goals to their one
And there began my adventure, made friends with everyone

The London Owls were soon formed, we came from everywhere
To follow our team through thick and thin, in weather foul or fair
The pleasure we would enjoy so much, whenever our team won
And even if we lost the game, we tried to have some fun

It was exciting travelling around, whether by train, coach or car
Watching our team playing, nowhere was too far
Many thought us mad, supporting a team over a hundred miles away
Though we remained passionate about our club known as 'the Wednesday'

Several years have passed since then, with times both good and bad
And whenever we were relegated, we all felt oh so sad
But none of us can ever forget, promotion and winning at Wembley
We're Wednesdayites until we die, as good as family

Our mascot is the owl, whose reputation is wise
Whenever our ground is full, the sound made is no surprise
Here's to all our loyal fans, wherever we reside
Let's hope we see more glory days, and support our team with pride

Astounding
Written 3rd May 2016

How could they possibly win it?
The same was written about Greece
In the European Nations Finals of 2004
Beating Portugal, the hosts, twice if you please

Their odds were 100/1 and more
No surprise as they had never won a thing
No-one expected them to beat the very best
The Greeks took to the streets to dance and sing

We've had shocks in the FA Cup too
With finals won by the complete underdog
The likes of Sunderland, Wimbledon and Wigan recently
Which left most of us all agog

But none of these come even close
To the most astounding achievement of all
Leicester City were 5000/1 to be champions
Before any team had kicked a ball

Managed by the quiet Italian
Claudio Ranieri is his name
He put together a squad virtually unknown
But ready to play the game

They were soon at the top of the league
Having nearly been relegated last time around
And in the ex non-league Jamie Vardy
A superstar goal-scorer had been found

He had great support around him
With Mahrez, Drinkwater and the rest of the crew
While Kasper Schmeichel was as solid as a rock
And the opposition found it hard to break through

They are deserved champions with two games to spare
And the celebrations have already begun
An automatic entry to the Champion's League
Who says that can't be won?

It is refreshing when anyone succeeds for the very first time
Defying all the odds and logic too
Respect to Leicester City known as the Foxes
And to all their supporters in blue

Branston (Part 1)

Written 11th November 2015
As featured in "Animal Antics" and "Perfect Pets"

It was the beginning of September
We visited Battersea Dog's Home for the day
The very first time we saw Branston
A chocolate Labrador puppy found as a stray

He entered the room playfully
Boisterous and continually wagging his tail
Greeted us and then played with some toys
He was an excitable young male

We took him home in our car
As he looked curiously around
His grey-green eyes so shiny
Though he never made a sound

He soon found his favourite chair
And he was a real livewire
He'd suddenly jump up and bound around
And never seemed to tire

He had an appetite so huge
He'd eat anything within reach
We knew it was going to take time
There was so much for us to teach

A couple of months down the line
With a nearby park for him to roam
He eats, he plays, he sleeps content
And he's happy to have a good home

Branston (Part 2)

Written 19th February 2017

Branston has been living with us
For eighteen months and is no longer small
He's grown in stature and remains a handful
Though we wouldn't swap him at all

He's chocolate and gold with some white patches
A Siberian Husky crossbreed, so nimble on his feet
Very observant and always looking around
To see if there is a cat or fox in the street

He's playful and loves to stalk squirrels
And will wait and then pounce suddenly
Need to hold on to his lead so he doesn't reach them
Otherwise they will be just history

He eats for England always ready for more
And will follow any plate around the house
He's eaten part of the furniture where he sleeps
And always on the look-out for a rat or a mouse

He's a joy to own and loves to greet everyone
Brings a smile with his head out of the car window
He even won a competition for the most handsome hound
And is the happiest rescue dog we will ever know

The Cat
Written 22nd April 2016

Purring softly, observing all
Suddenly jumping, careful not to fall
Inquisitive, confident and loves to roam
Playful whether outside, or whether at home
Always protective, of its food and drink
Certainly much smarter than you think
Can see in the dark through its piercing eyes
Is unflappable around insects and even flies
Be careful of its paws, as they can scratch
Has an independence no other pet can match
Can be different colours and sizes, but never fat
Welcome to the world of the cat

Our Rabbit

Written 29th July 2013

Our rabbit is a lionhead, we've had her from two months old
She's a character, playful, inquisitive and sometimes very bold
She makes us happy wherever she goes, certainly so tame
Her ears prick up every time, when we call her name

She loves to munch her nuggets and plenty of fresh hay
Her life is spent eating and resting, though she mainly wants to play
It's funny to watch her bunny-hop in the garden during the day
She runs so fast and jumps over anything standing in her way

She's spoilt as she has her own hutch and a cage for indoors too
If you give her one of her favourite treats she's always pleased with you
She loves her carrots and broccoli, while bananas and raspberries are a treat
She tidies up both her homes and likes to keep them neat

When our daughter plays the violin she seems to respond with joy
To the piano too, as she rustles around, playing with her favourite toy
She's very aware and always knows when it's time to come inside
As we chase her around the garden she knows exactly where to hide

We are lucky to have such a wonderful pet and hope she stays safe and sound
When she is outside we need to keep a close watch, as there may be foxes
around
She's a ray of sunshine and very much a part of our family
We couldn't swap her for any other, our rabbit called Danny

The Bird, Cat and Dog Trilogy

Written 10th August 2016

Beautiful...a sight to behold
Independent...self-sufficient whether it is hot or cold
Roaming...travels far and wide
Diving...swoops to conquer and rarely denied

Curious...curiosity killed the cat
Athletic...jumps over this and that
Taunting...eyes focused on a mouse or rat

Demanding...especially for walks or food
Obedient...after training is usually good
Growling...shows feelings when in a mood

Bear With Me

Written 20th January 2012
(Can be sung to the tune of Abide With Me)

Please bear with me....bear with me you will see
I'm trying to help you....won't you bear with me?
I won't be long.....just hear my song for free
I'll make you happy....if you bear with me

One thing you should know....there isn't long to go
Life is full of waiting.....queuing to and fro
Ask yourself this question....why must it be?
Every time I phone I'm told...please bear with me

So, what's the point...in complaining every time?
You're driven crazy....by that dreadful line
One day you'll realise...it was meant to be
No matter who you are....just bear with me!

Chocolate

Written 30th October 2012
Published in The Poet Tree – A Collection of Poetry

Isn't it the most wonderful thing ever made?
Your memories as a child never fade
Do you remember when you took your very first bite?
We gobbled up our chocolate whether dark or light

It brings so much pleasure to all around
Whether it's inside a packet or bought by the pound
Your eyes light up if someone gives you a box
Who can say no to such a vast choice of chocs?

It is the best form of comfort your money can buy
You just can't resist some, no matter how hard you try
There are so many flavours, just take your pick
Enjoy your time consuming it, whether thin or thick

Be sure your eyes aren't bigger than your stomach in one go
There are three square meals a day, more important as you know
Though if by chance you leave any food on your plate
I hope the reason isn't eating too much chocolate

Tea or Coffee?

Written 5th April 2016

Tea or coffee?
Sugar or saccharine?
Milk or juice?
Butter or margarine?

White bread or brown bread?
Honey or jam?
Pasta or pizza?
Cheese or ham?

White meat or red meat?
Salt or pepper?
Fried fish or grilled fish?
Oil or vinegar?

Black olives or green olives?
Cucumber or tomato?
Beans or peas?
Chips or baked potato?

White wine or red wine?
Orange or lemon?
Sparkling water or still water?
Grapes or melon?

Apple or banana?
Ice cream or jelly?
Cake or biscuits?
Tea or coffee?

The Numbers Game
Written 19th February 2015

When we think of one
It rhymes with fun
Then when there's two
There's more that we can do
A crowd they say is three
Though we enjoy breakfast, lunch and tea
And as we move to four
We're always wanting more
Next comes five
It's so good to be alive
How about six
There's nothing we can't fix
Then we reach seven
Surely there's a heaven
Then follows eight
Better early than late
Moving on to nine
Don't worry we'll be fine
And finally there's ten
Go back and start again

Farewell Barry

Written 18th November 2013 in memory of Barry Williams who worked in
Business Travel until he was 70 years old

So, finally, you've taken your very last ever call
And leave HRG with pride and certainly no fall
I'm sure you remember your time here, both the good and the bad
As you wipe away a tear, perhaps a little sad

No further hassles to really make you frown
Though no matter what you were faced with, nothing got you down
We'll remember your chirpy manner, always a smile on your face
And when the clock chimed five you left without a trace

So farewell Barry, we wish you the very best
And many years to come of peace and good rest
Don't forget your friends here working hard as you know
And if you're ever passing, be sure to come and say hello

CRY

138

5th April 1986

In loving memory of my father 04/12/23 - 05/04/86
Written 28th March 2013
As featured in Forward Poetry " A Day In The Life"

The 5th April 1986 is a day I can never ever forget
It was Grand National day and, as usual, I had placed my bet
I picked three horses and would you believe it they were first, third and fourth
West Tip, Mr Snugfit and Classified, though I was heading north

To watch my team, Sheffield Wednesday, play against the Everton
A place in a Wembley final at stake, and the sun so brightly shone
That we lost in extra-time was really not my concern
Because in the morning the worst news possible I was about to learn

A phone call from Cyprus to greet me as I woke
An uncle calling, I could hear his tears even before he spoke
He was calling about his brother, my father, taken in the night
He'd had a heart-attack before, but had recovered and felt alright

This time there was no sign it would happen again so soon
My eyes filling with water, as I gazed up at the moon
It really couldn't dawn on me, I would never see him again
I felt numb with shock and thought of my mother's pain

She was in Cyprus with my younger brother, who has Down's syndrome
So many thoughts rushed through my brain, if only they had stayed home
My father's wish had always been, to die in the place of his birth
He often said life was sweet and short, and always knew its worth

On the spin of a coin, he came to England in 1951
It could have been South Africa, and a life so full of sun
Though I was pleased to be born here, for England is the best
So much history and greenery, and raised in London's West

He was a hairdresser by trade, and soon opened his shop
Was respected by the neighbourhood, as he made it to the top
Was on the local chamber of commerce, and met the prime minister
His unisex satisfied everyone, whether a him or a her

He used to play backgammon and cards, always determined to win
He may have gambled too much at times, though who is without sin?
I'll never forget him playing his recorder, and he loved to sing
He did his utmost to encourage me to do well in everything

At the end of that so tragic day, I went to catch the plane
Knowing that my life would never be the same again
When I saw my mother and brother we hugged and shared the tears
He was sixty-two, we clung to the memories over all the years

And now all these years later, I remember that day so well
When my father, a passionate man, met his final bell
His picture still upon my wall, he remains a part of me
My only regret, the grand-children he never got to see

Mum

In loving memory of my mother 11.07.23 - 13.01.99
Written 9th March 2015

My mum's life was an amazing story
She was the second youngest of six children
She grew up in Cyprus leading a sheltered life
And was kept far away from all men

She lived in the mountains of Mandria
Though sometimes went into Limassol town
She was very pretty and always smiling
Though never allowed to walk alone

My dad was a hairdresser working there
And one day their eyes should meet
They fell in love very quickly
As Dad swept her off her feet

Her parents had heard he liked to gamble
And so did not approve of him
Dad knew his chances of marrying her
Would always be very slim

Incredibly they eloped and ran away
Were married and began their life
My older brother, Nick, was born
And my dad had the very best wife

In 1951 he decided it was time to change
Leave Cyprus and move elsewhere
He spun a coin, heads for England, tails South Africa
It was heads so he headed there

My mum could hardly speak any English
As she arrived with Nick six months later
Dad had set up a hairdressing business
Clearly better than being a waiter

142

By the time we reached 1961
My younger brother and I had been born
Though Michael had Down's syndrome
And our lives became so forlorn

Mum was so hard-working and clean
The house was spotless every day
She groomed the three of us to look so smart
And was motherly in her own special way

The Greek food she cooked was sumptuous
My favourite dolmades were so filling
Though when she took us to the dentist and opticians
Michael and I were not so willing

She was also very religious
Took us to church most Sundays each year
The neighbours always admired her
Her face always natural and full of cheer

Sadly the stress became too much for the family
With Dad gambling and Mum's constant care for Michael
There were often arguments and sometimes violence
Mum would be crying and we'd be upset as well

Eventually Mum had a stroke in her fifties
Then diabetes followed as well
Her final five years spent in a wheelchair
She knew the difference between heaven and hell

And now she is at rest with the angels
She was a mum in a million for me
Her memory lives on forever in my heart
And a grand-daughter she never lived to see

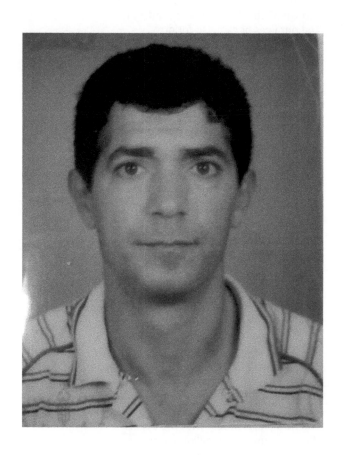

Brother Nick

In loving memory of my older brother 15.03.47 - 22.04.16
Published in A Collection of Poetry - Immersed in Word 13.05.16

Panicos Evzonas was born in Cyprus
On the 15th March 1947
He was brought to England aged five
When our father tossed a coin for London or Durban

He was the only foreign kid in his school
But learnt English in a flash
Improved our parents knowledge of it
As our father opened a barber's shop to make his cash

I was born and Panicos, known as Nick, was happy
To have a much younger brother
Though he began to become mischievous
And would receive the slipper from our mother

He was attentive to me at all times
And would always include me at play
Whether football, horse-racing, backgammon or chess
Made me competitive day by day

We played Subbuteo, Totopoly and other board games
Monopoly, Cleudo and Risk too
His favourite horse Mill House, mine Arkle
His team Forest in red, and mine Wednesday in blue

He played in goal for Parkside Football Team
Even though he was shorter than five foot eight
He was fearless and always determined
And friends found him a very good mate

He would listen to Pick of the Pops on the radio
Introduced me to the Beatles, Rolling Stones and the rest
He wasn't either a mod or a rocker
John Lennon saying he was a mocker was best

We saw the Rolling Stones live in concert
In the hot summer of 1969
He promoted their songs in his record shop
Though father had another job for him in mind

He followed him into the hairdressing business
And would cut my hair and our younger brother's too
I remember he would reward me with chocolates
When I ran him an errand or two

I was frustrated that he started smoking
And always wanted him to stop
He would give me money to buy his newspaper
And cigarettes from the local shop

He was married three times over
And divorced from every wife
Sadly had no children of his own
Though he certainly lived his life

Saw his beloved Nottingham Forest at Wembley
And took me with him in 1990 when they won
That summer we went to Royal Ascot
Wearing Disney character hats and having fun

We had the same sense of humour
Reciting lines from favourite movies we had seen
Sometimes laughing ourselves silly
Whether it was Fawlty Towers, Black Adder or Mr Bean

He retired to Cyprus when in his fifties
And enjoyed the relaxed lifestyle there
But missed England and its variety
And returned despite warmer weather being rare

His best catchphrase was always the same
"Wants are many, needs are few"
He was proud of his Spartan origins
Though he gave away much it is true

We shared good times and bad times
And saw both our parents pass away
Helped our younger brother with Down's syndrome
To cope with life each day

So farewell brother Nick
You are finally laid to rest
As far as brothers go in this life
You were certainly one of the best

Brother Michael
Written 22nd June 2016

Michael Evzona was born in 1960 on 4th June
Unusually born with Down's syndrome
Our mother suffered greatly with his birth
And he was finally delivered at home

We loved him immediately and he was so different
With a gorgeous smile on his face
He loved to play and often laughed
Was a child of God and always wanted to embrace

He was hard work for our mother
As she did everything she could do
We were a close-knit family with Greek Orthodox beliefs
And often went to church too

He loved his sport especially football and horse-racing
And we played cricket in the park behind our house
We would wrestle together sometimes
Or play hide and seek like a cat and mouse

He enjoyed going on the coach to the day centre
To be with others who were similar to him
Sometimes mischievously set off the fire alarm
And could be naughty, but would never swim

He used to sweep up the hair in our father's shop
Always polite to customers saying 'hello' and 'goodbye'
Loved going to the Wimpy Bar for a special grill
His favourite food was Greek, and with Mums' cooking we know why

He would sing along to his favourite songs
Mainly David Bowie and the Rolling Stones because of me
Our older brother tried to have him support Nottingham Forest
But I won that battle and his team was Sheffield Wednesday

I took him to football matches and the horse races too
We had great days out, especially if we won
Our family made sure he enjoyed his life
And holidays to Cyprus were so much fun

Our father even once drove him from London to Cyprus
Stopping at various places along the way
I couldn't go with them as I was working
Though I regret it to this very day

He never understood our parents passing away
And became upset a lot of the time, unable to cope
With not seeing or being hugged by them ever again
To keep him as healthy as I could was my only hope

He shared a house with his friend Stephen and live-in carer
When he finally left home aged forty-one years
Though he was only three roads away from me
So I could see him regularly to avoid many tears

Sadly dementia set in and he's moved to a nursing home
He's distressed, often shouting, having good days and bad
He has become wheelchair-bound, and not the Michael I knew
I don't want him to suffer, and feel so sad

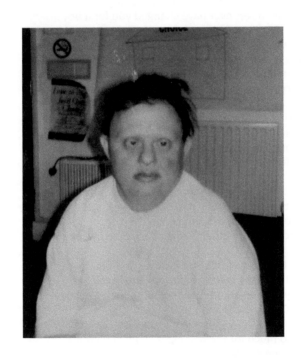

Katerina

Written 12th October 2012 dedicated to my first-born child
Published in Light Up The Dark - A Collection of Poetry

Dear Katerina Andrea, you were my first born
I held you so close, as your cord was torn
You really brought me so many tears of joy
And I would never ever have changed you for a boy

I rocked you to sleep, holding you so tight
And would always wake for you if you cried in the night
Your sparkling brown eyes, shining so very bright
And carrying you everywhere, as you were so light

It was so sad for both of us, when you were taken away
Having been so used to you, every night and day
Even though my marriage had failed and was no more
I would fight to see you by using the law

I fought through the courts to make rightly sure
That you would be on my passport, so we could travel more
Our time was so limited, I felt so much pain
And lived for every other weekend, I would see you again

I did my best to give you so much joy and fun
We went to many places, enjoying time in the sun
You've probably forgotten where we went on holiday
Cyprus, Dubai, Brazil and the USA

We did so much for the first eight years of your life
Though time was passing me by, then I took a new wife
My dream was that we would all truly get along
Though I knew, whatever I tried, I would just be wrong

Alexandra was born and my life was changed again
It grieved me to limit our contact, though I know you felt more pain
I'm sorry I abandoned you, compared to how we'd been before
I tried to stay in your life, and wish I had done more

Her type 1 Diabetes just made life more unfair
The stress and the pressure for you, I was nowhere
Though I thought of you day and night, praying you would be strong
No matter what you were going through, and to know your right from wrong

I was so very proud that you did so well at school
And to go to university, you proved nobody's fool
And now the world's your oyster, and I pray your dreams come true
Just remember you were my first born, there'll never be another you

Reaching Sixty

Written 26th March 2015 on the very day of my 60th Birthday
As featured in Forward Poetry "Over The Page"

Reaching sixty is a major milestone
Even in this day and age
I remember how different life was in the 1960s
When there was no such thing as road rage

When I was a child it was very exciting
To play Monopoly, Totopoly and Subbuteo
Enjoy television despite its limited transmission
There was still time for Backgammon and Cluedo

I loved playing football, tennis and running in the park
Had many friends in infants and junior school
My dad encouraged me to do well in my subjects
I did well though sometimes played the fool

Achieved a place in grammar school of which I was proud
To mix with other brains of the borough
Languages were my forte and history too
I made sure my homework was thorough

I played for the school football team
Was cross-country and chess champion too
Won the Greenford under 18s tennis singles twice
And how my teenage years flew

I loved performing on the stage
Singing Rolling Stones songs with the school band
And always ready to play a prank
Sometimes totally unplanned

I left school and went into banking
My maths was always ahead of the rest
I was number one cashier at Lloyds branches
Though having weekends off was really the best

I switched jobs and joined British Airways
My parents were so very proud
Travel concessions for the family everywhere
Though we were just part of a very large crowd

I started doing stand-up comedy and wrote poems
Nothing really fazed me
At work events or friend's functions
And most of the time performed for free

I married, divorced and married again
And have two lovely daughters to show
Have been through much pain and pleasure
Experiencing life's high and low

I was often on the BBC radio
Talking about Sheffield Wednesday and smoking too
Trying to encourage people to stop or never start
And appeared on TV for scrabble and a quiz too

I have worked in Business Travel
For the past twenty five years
Been lucky enough to travel far and wide
Found it easier to cope with any fears

I am on the Greenford 365 website
For my fundraising since 1994
Have run in four London marathons
Several BUPA 10k races and more

My family and friends are here today
Many of you have known me most of my life
Let's drink a toast to the next ten years
And thanks for putting up with me to my wife

The Loneliness of the Marathon Runner

Written 25th March 2007 in memory of the four London Marathons
I ran in 1994, 2000, 2005, 2007

So you've decided to train , all alone
Time will tell, you should have known
It's hard to please, all around you
When you've committed, to what you're going through

The first steps are easy, though you mustn't rush
As you make your way, just a silent hush
You can hear your feet, as they pound the ground
Before you know it, you've gone once round

The park is as safe, a place to train
Whether sun or cloud, wind or rain
Each lap done, makes a mile
Greet each passer-by, with a smile

You'll see children, having fun
Dogs off their leash, so they can run
Shoppers returning, each carrying a bag
Someone sitting on a bench, just having a fag

The wonder of nature, is all around
Squirrels climbing trees, worms on the ground
Birds chirping loudly, way up on high
Oh what joy, it must be to fly

Shouts of encouragement, always nice to hear
'You'll be alright, have no fear'
No pain no gain, so they say
After ten miles slog, it's just another day

You think of family, loved ones and friends
Life in general, how, why, and when?
This is all worthwhile, you convince yourself for sure
Come the day of the race, you'll feel more secure

Only Dextro to suck, and help you on your way
No marshalls on route, no water today
You see a lady moving, in her mobile chair
You're lucky to be running, wish life could be more fair

And as you begin, you're welcome final lap
You've done so very well, give yourself a clap
Even better just to know, your charity will thank you
For giving up your time, make someone's dream come true

The relief is there to see, as you reach your door
Ring the bell, home at last, one thing is for sure
You may have been lonely, running on your own
But family spoils you, drink and a bath, now you're not alone

Ordeal and Relief

Written 24th April 2007
Published in "A Day In Time"

Marathon day has come and gone
A day we'll never forget
We showed our determination, all day long
Are we glad we did, you bet!

The weather wasn't very kind
Whilst we jostled at the start
The sun beat down, was it in our mind?
We might just fall apart

The klaxon sounded, away we went
Encouraged by the roar
The first mile run, we knew this meant
Just twenty five miles more

Plenty of water for us to drink
The helpers did their best
There wasn't time for us to think
Of peace and quiet and rest

The people gathered round the streets
Often calling our name
Children handing out their sweets
We took them, oh the shame!!

The temperature rose, and made us sweat
We prayed for cloud or rain
The whole ordeal, made us fret
And slowly we felt the pain

Still we heard the praise and cheers
As we reached the final miles
Through it all, the laughter and tears
The support of all those smiles

The sadness felt as many fell
Trying to achieve their aim
To make their charity's cash flow swell
They knew this was no game

And so at last the final straight
With no more of the grief
To pass the line, and get our time
It's over, what a relief

London Bupa 10K

Written 1st June 2011 in memory of the
several races I ran raising funds for Cancer and Diabetes

Today was the day, for the London Bupa 10K
Though the sun was shining, far too bright,
Over eight thousand runners, down at the start,
Everyone of us, hemmed in tight,
Among others I saw Mo Farah and Paula Radcliffe,
Though would I see them during the race, as if

We jostled for position, many of us wearing our logos,
For the charities we came to support,
The course before us was past magnificent landmarks,
Though once running, we barely gave them a thought

I ran with my zebra puppet glove, wearing a smile,
Encouraged by so many, on route
The bands played along, some burst into song,
And I heard the occasional hoot

With the sun beating down, there was relief all around,
When we ran through the showers so cool,
Took water on board as I ran with the hoard,
Though I would be nobody's fool

It was amazing to think Mo was finished, having a drink,
As I passed the sign saying 6K,
No matter, I would go on and complete my run,
Even if it took me all day

So the finish in sight, I ran with all my might,
To complete as fast as I could,
Fifty minutes wasn't bad, considering I had,
Not trained, and that wasn't good

Now all that's left to do, is to thank you and you,
For sponsoring, so many who ran,
For various charities all trying our best,
To raise, as much as we can

Hillsborough Ninety-Six
Written 27th April 2016

Hillsborough stadium was always famous
For many years it had seen the very best
Home to Sheffield Wednesday with a large capacity
Any away team knew they were in for a test

It had hosted several matches in the World Cup
And countless FA Cup semi finals too
And a League Cup Final replay in '77
Between Villa and Everton in blue

The Seventies and Eighties were fraught with crowd trouble
As opposition gangs would roam
Fighting outside and inside grounds
It happened whether playing away or at home

The government's solution was to build fences
And keep fans caged in a pen
Stop them going on to the pitch
Though it was only a matter of time when

Overcrowding became an issue
Especially when the top clubs played
Though the 15th April 1989 was a tragedy
Made even worse by the safety barricade

Liverpool played Forest in the FA Cup semi final
A sunny day as the ground filled fast
Sadly for ninety six Liverpool supporters
This day would be their last

Why weren't they given the Spion Kop end
Which could hold over twice as many fans
Instead of being crammed into the Leppings Lane
Where police had other plans

As the tragedy started to unfold
People caught in the crush with no escape
Many trying to clamber over the fence
Their lives mattered far more than any red tape

As panic set in and children cried
At the disturbing reality of it all
Many bodies covered just lying on the pitch
This was supposed to be a match of football

Many more had been injured in the mayhem
Though thank God they were still alive
Fellow fans doing their best to help
As they waited for ambulances to arrive

This was the worst nightmare ever seen
At a venue everyone knew so well
Emotions ran high as police and fans blamed each other
There seemed no end to this living hell

Ninety-six genuine fans lost their lives
And some newspapers must hold their heads in shame
There certainly was a deceitful cover-up
And it took 27 years to admit who was to blame

It really could have happened to any of us
We learn from our mistakes and atone
Time is the healer of all wounds
And together we'll never walk alone

Slaughter of the Innocents
Written 18th July 2016

'Slaughter of the Innocents' ran the headline
We are in the 21st century and nothing has changed
Life, although precious, can be meaningless for some
Especially any fanatics, and anyone deranged

BC used to stand for 'before Christ'
Though 'before computers' seems more appropriate now
Many have turned their backs on true religion
How is mankind supposed to survive somehow?

Mind-control is there for all to see
No-one is safe whether they are young or old
Chaos and destruction all over the world
How can men's hearts remain so cold?

It's a no-win situation, which has no end
What's the difference whether we suffer or just die?
Tyranny, revenge or insanity all the same
Man will never change or even try

The suffering goes on amidst all the tears
Why do we have to endure this life of shame?
Children poisoned by those intent on their control
If only it were just a game

Wind time forward a thousand years
Do you really believe it will be any different?
Just as it wasn't two thousand years ago
We need more than just a man who was heaven-sent

Fear

Written 16th November 2015

Fear is the word of the 21st century
Fear of the unknown every single day
Fear that you might be in the wrong place
Fear at the wrong time whether at work or play

Fear a fanatic is ready to cause mayhem
Fear he or she is ready to die for their so-called cause
Fear whether in the street, in a car, a bus or plane
Fear there is no protection despite all our laws

Fear for our babies, children and ourselves
Fear someone is deranged because of drugs they took
Fear that it could be a knife, a gun or suicide-bomber
Fear we can't see them no matter where we look

Fear follows us wherever we may go
Fear it haunts us until our dying day
Fear we wish it would just pass us by
Fear please let it not be us we pray

Defiance

Written 19th November 2015

'We will never surrender' said Winston Churchill
And that was over seventy-five years ago
His resolve and determination was inspirational
As we battled with our foe

Six long years were lost and all because
Of a madman with a crazy plan
To change the world and rule it all
Without any care for all the destruction

Many tyrants have come and gone
And many innocents suffered so much
We have to stay strong, no matter what
The invaders kill, take or touch

Time has taught us nothing ever changes
Hatred, jealousy and domination our fear
We must stand together and never lie down
And hold every life precious dear

And now we have another evil
With which we must contend
Terrorism and migration
Who is our enemy and who our friend

We must try to end this madness
Which could destroy us all
Show them our togetherness and defiance
And we will never fall

Do We See Them?
Written 4th March 2015

Every day when we walk down the street
Whether the weather is good or bad
There is a situation all around
Which should only make us sad

Why are there so many people on the street
Homeless and begging for money?
People ignore them and walk on by
While some even think it's funny

It's hard to know which ones you can trust
As some will try to cheat
Pretend they are homeless and pocket the cash
As police are rarely out on the beat

Though most are for real and just bad luck
Has left them in this terrible state
It could even happen to you or me
Life can turn and no-one can be sure of their fate

Some have sleeping bags and some just a box
While others may even be there with a pet
No respite for them if it's below freezing at night
When it rains, we know they'll be wet

It's crazy to think there are houses still
Empty in this world that we live
Why should anyone really be out on the street
When the wealthy have so much they could give?

The question we must all ask ourselves
Time and again, do we really care?
Some old, some young, both male and female
Do we 'really' notice them there?

Can You Hear Me?

Written 18th August 2014

From birth, there are those of us
Who are lucky to hear and see,
And we start chatting constantly
By the tender age of three

We're taught right and wrong at home
Before we first go to school,
And when we mix with other children
We don't want to be anyone's fool

We have happy times and sad times too
Wherever we might be,
And sometimes look up to heaven
Can you hear me?

We learn of life's cruelty
How nasty people can be,
Why should anyone suffer at all?
Can you hear me?

Some without a home
And others without food,
Are we going to be bad?
Or will we be good?

Surely we know it is just fate
As to where we are all born,
Some from happy families
While others are sadly torn

Some growing up
Playing and joking,
While others go down the path
Of drinking and smoking

Some end up mixing
With the wrong crowd,
While others are achievers
And always standing proud

We spend a whole lifetime
Trying to find a cure,
Put an end to people's suffering
All disease gone for evermore

There have always been so many
I wish the blind could see,
If you really are there
Can you hear me?

And the very worst of all
The never-ending world of war,
I hope that one day
There just won't be any more

Absence
Written 9th September 2015

Absence makes the heart grow fonder
Or is it out of sight out of mind?
People take each other for granted so easily
Though it is never better to be cruel to be kind

In today's world it is so easy
For anyone to get to know someone so far away
Those first moments of chatting and flirting
And brightening up an otherwise empty day

Though it takes two to understand each other
And learn what makes each other tick
To discover if they really are on the same wave-length
There are so many from whom to pick

And in time you become closer together
Confiding more and more each day
The flirtation can become oh so strong
And the words become easier to say

But when you are apart for whatever reason
As life is full of its ups and downs
Don't let the absence bring you stress
Time is the healer of all wounds

So embrace the adventure from day one
With all its pleasures and its pain
Never take any situation for granted
Life remains a learning curve again and again

2014
Written 16th December 2014

Exactly a hundred years since the start
Of the horrendous First World War
What was it all about really
And did we think there would be any more?

This year has seen a new terror
Making us all feel insecure
The Islamic State is fanatical
And no-one is safe for sure

The sadness of so many left
Without shelter, water or food
The young, the old, the brave and bold
Whether their hearts are bad or good

Ebola was the latest disease
To scare us as it spread
Life has so many different illnesses
Which leave so many dead

Millions remain homeless on our planet
How can this possibly continue?
There are many empty houses to be found
We know there's more we can do

Yet still we strive to search
For any life form elsewhere
With another mission into outer space
Do the scientists really care?

About the suffering here on earth
Which never has an end
We should show humanity and help each other
Everyone needs a friend

The smiles are there for all to see
From those wealthy celebrities
Whether from business, sport, entertainment or inheritance
They can mostly do as they please

So will there be an improvement?
In the next hundred years, will we learn at all?
Eradicate wars, diseases and homelessness worldwide
Live peacefully until our final call

Armageddon

Written 9th February 2016

Aggressive
Ruthless
Murderous
Angry
Godless
Exterminating
Dangerous
Despairing
Obnoxious
Nothing

So Final
Written 2nd October 2014 dedicated to the
sad passing away of 14-year-old Alice Gross R.I.P

Why does anyone have to die so young?
Being chosen or just unlucky who knows
So much agony for family and friends
Life has its highs, but certainly its lows

A young girl who had so much talent to share
A twinkle in her eye, a smile upon her face
Taken from us in a moment of sheer madness
As exhausted police search every place

Where there's life, there's still always a chance
We pray she's alive and still cling to hope
Please don't let her suffer in any way
Or just be found, hanging on a rope

What makes any person become so heartless
To have the power to take someone away
Through force or just playing with their mind?
And a terrible price for the family to pay

Does such a young life deserve such a fate?
They're just a child with so much to give
Playing, dancing, singing, or running around
Why should it end before they fully live?

The sadness as the reality of it all dawns
Where once was hope now we can only mourn
The punishment can never fit the crime
No wonder we question why some were ever born